£14.99

EDUCATION MANAGEMENT SERIES

Series Editor: John Sayer

Towards self-managing schools

Cassell

Wellington House
125 Strand
London WC2R 0BB

387 Park Avenue South
New York
NY 10016–8810

British Library Cataloguing-in-Publication Data
A catalogue record for this book is available from the British Library.

ISBN 0–304–32982–7 (hardback)
       0–304–32984–3 (paperback)

Phototypeset by Intype, London
Printed and bound in Great Britain by Redwood Books, Trowbridge, Wiltshire

Contents

Foreword by the series editor

For many reasons, it is important to capture the personal experiences of leading actors in the initial and transition stages of major change. The early years of the 1990s marked a radical change in the way British schools were to be run. Some had already negotiated and piloted, for educational and professional reasons, individual moves towards self-managing schools, but it is arguable that they were no more prepared for the politically driven and imposed changes than those who had watched and waited.

All the writers in this book, whether or not they have perceived benefits to the education of children in such elements of self-management as site-based financial management of resources or staff appraisal, are looking for ways to improve what has now been set up by post-1986 legislation. In their proposals, there are the elements of change not only for a future government's programme but also for those directly responsible for managing schools. It was with the secondary sector that local management of schools began, and that is the focus here, to be followed, we hope, by a study of the experiences and needs of self-managing primary schools.

The title itself poses a challenge: are we in fact moving towards self-managing schools, or is this the new emperor's clothing which one writer observed in his former LEA? Can schools, which have recently had to accept standardized national packages of curriculum, assessment, appraisal and inspection schemes, and ceiling-high regulations, really be seen to be more self-managing than in previous dispensations? Similarly, within schools, are teachers, whether as teams or as individuals, more self-managing in a professional sense, or have we been turned back to the era in which a Colonel Blimp could say, 'I stand for no interference with the right of the Indians to do as they are damn well told'? Is even the language of the market economy no more than a cloak for central government intervention, fragmentation of local opposition and deadening regulation? What use is choice of school – even if there were more choice than before – if it is merely a choice of the shop from which to buy a regulated standardized product? Where is the evidence of greater parental influence on either political or professional actions?

The answers depend, as they always have done, on the ability of schools and communities to work out their priorities, not to be dominated from inside or outside, and to select those elements of change, such as school development planning or negotiated records of achievement, which lend themselves to positive improvement. In doing so, the messages which run through all these different chapters are consistent: imposed change does not work; people have to be engaged in a shared pursuit of common goals; that simply has not happened to the education system in the period being described here; and it must begin to happen right away.

This book draws out structured reflection from live experiences and concludes with an invitation to examine the complex concepts underlying the differences between management and leadership, not least through a disciplined scrutiny of followership. This is the message which has still to reach government, but it is also the message vital to the future of school communities. Whilst some chapters will be most appreciated as a record of what has been happening, there is much here which can be related to the priorities for the future laid out in the four most recent books in the Education Management series. Together, it is hoped they may contribute strongly to policy and practice through which to enter the new millennium.

John Sayer

Preface

In 1632, when reviewing changes in schooling during the early decades of the seventeenth century, Comenius concluded that: 'For more than a hundred years much complaint has been made of the unmethodical way in which schools are conducted, but it is only within the last thirty years that any serious attempt has been made to find a remedy for this state of things. And with what result? Schools remain exactly as they were' (*The Great Didactic*).

Prior to the Education Reform Act of 1988 many had believed that this was also an enduring twentieth-century perception of schools and that little had really changed during the preceding thirty years: that underneath all the rhetoric of the comprehensive reform of the 1960s secondary education had perpetuated the traditions of the former grammar schools, in that what was valued above all else was academic achievement; that the Great Debate of the late 1970s had marginally excited a few politicians but no one in schools; and that only the consequences of demographic decline in the early 1980s and financial constraints through government 'capping' of LEA expenditure had produced ripples of change in the life and work of schools. However, during the last decade mandated programmes of reform in school governance, organization and curriculum and determined thrusts away from provider-led to client-focused policies appear to have relegated the insights of Comenius to the voluminous catalogue of historical perceptions of education.

In an attempt to characterize an understanding that education in schools *has* undergone major change, this book was conceived as a contribution to the tracing of the early development of self-managing secondary schools in England and Wales. At the core of that development is the legislative watershed in school management provided by the 1988 Education Act. From 1989 when the initial sections of this Act were triggered, the structure, organization and culture of schooling in England and Wales have been in a process of fundamental and dynamic change.

The ways in which schools have adapted to these changes are the foci of this book – not least to record how headteachers and their colleagues in secondary schools have traversed unfamiliar pathways across new curricular and administrative landscapes. Of course, it is impossible to chart ways in which all schools have adapted to processes of unavoidable change and it is not claimed that the particular experiences of the schools included in this book are typical of all secondary schools. Nevertheless, it is believed that much of their recent experience reflects ways in which many schools have adjusted to localized self-managing responsibilities in the provision of education. Further, and because of the pace of change and the pragmatic political roller-coaster momentum, these schools provide a perspective of change in school governance that might otherwise be forgotten or overlooked within a relatively short time. Not least important are the headlong political drive towards local management autonomy within planned emaciation of LEA frameworks and the establishment of a new grant-maintained schools sector under burgeoning central government control. These are, or should be, matters of both contemporary and future interest.

For example, and because of the pace of government legislative and regulatory change, the perspectives offered in this book, which was compiled during the summer and autumn of 1993, will almost certainly have been overtaken by events and other government episodic pronouncements by the date of its publication. In itself, the book will provide an indicator of the brief shelf-life of some government education strategies and the government's pot-noodle style of policy-making, devoid of consultation with those who are required to implement fundamental educational innovation in our schools for the presumed benefit of millions of pupils.

Although others will undoubtedly hold different opinions, it is held that it is currently impossible to provide a dispassionate, objective and balanced view of the sweeping changes in the education system of England and Wales mandated assiduously by various versions of Conservative governments since 1979. In an attempt to provide a measure of understanding of major recent and current systemic reforms, this book offers an introductory review of some of the outcomes of central government strategies and an exploration of the themes of increasing government intervention and control in the education system.

Vivian Williams
Oxford, 1994

Notes on contributors

BRIGID BEATTIE has been Principal of Burntwood Grant-maintained Girls' Comprehensive School, Wandsworth, since 1986. The school's mission statement is 'The best education today for the women of tomorrow'. She is a Fellow of the Management Centre, Roehampton College of Education; a member of the BBC Council for Education Broadcasting; and a member of the Department for Education Steering Committee for a project on bullying being undertaken in Sheffield. She is also a Fellow of the Royal Society of Arts, a non-executive director of Wandsworth Community Health Trust and a member of the council of Understanding British Industry (UBI).

DAVID CHURCH taught in Slough before entering educational administration in the then Rotherham County Borough in 1966. Subsequently he held senior education officer posts in Swindon, Wiltshire and Oxfordshire and latterly in Oxfordshire LEA as a senior adviser.

PAUL COTTER taught in LEA grammar and comprehensive schools in Manchester, Salford and North Yorkshire before his appointment in 1985 as Headteacher of Tewkesbury School, Gloucestershire. During the mid-1970s he enjoyed a year's sabbatical at Manchester University leading to the Diploma in Educational Guidance. This was followed by further research into study habits and attitudes leading to the award of an M.Ed.

MICHAEL FOSSEY taught in Westmorland followed by an appointment as Senior Lecturer (in Chemistry and Education) at St Martin's College, Lancaster, for seven years before returning to teaching in Carlisle. Following appointments as Deputy Head (Workington) and Acting Head (Whitehaven), he was appointed to establish Stainburn School in Workington, Cumbria, as part of a major reorganization. Now in its tenth year, OFSTED inspectors have concluded that 'Stainburn is a good school'.

DAVID HILL has been inspector of schools for sixteen years and has been involved in many educational changes during that time-span. Previously he taught all age groups from reception to adult students in a variety of settings including a spell as headteacher of two schools – in Leicestershire and York-shire. He is especially interested in the development of the curriculum for the middle years and in educational administration. He is a Fellow of the Royal Society of Arts.

JOHN HOWELLS taught in a range of schools from independent to secondary modern in Birmingham, on the Sussex coast and in West Africa. He has been a secondary head in Oxfordshire for more than twenty years, the past thirteen as Head of Chipping Norton Secondary School.

DAVID MARTIN is Head of Chenderit School, Middleton Cheney, near Banbury, and Convener of the National Co-ordinating Committee on Learning and Assessment (NCCLA). He held earlier appointments as deputy head and head in Hertfordshire and Northamptonshire as well as teacher-tutor at the University of London Institute of Education in its History Department, has lectured widely and has organized conferences in the UK, Europe and the USA. He is a founding member of the TEMPUS higher education project, 'Developing Schools for Democracy in Europe', based at the University of Oxford.

ED MCCONNELL taught in inner-city schools in Liverpool and London before moving to Oxfordshire in 1973. After a decade as a senior year tutor and deputy head he moved to his first headship in 1984. His present appointment as headteacher of The Marlborough School at Woodstock began in 1986. The main focus of his interest has been curriculum management, but he has also devoted much time to developments in the recording of pupil achievement and plays a leading role in the Oxford Consortium for Educational Achievement.

VIVIAN WILLIAMS taught in Cheshire and Liverpool before entering educational administration. Following service as an education officer in two county LEAs and as Deputy Chief Education Officer in a city LEA, he was appointed as University Lecturer in Educational Studies (Governance) at the University of Oxford Department of Educational Studies. He is also a Fellow of St Peter's College and Director of the Norham Centre for Leadership Studies – an international centre for management studies and leadership development. Recent publications include *Adult Education and Social Purpose* (1988), *Schools and External Relations: Managing the New Partnerships* (co-editor, 1989) and *Reforming Education in a Changing World: International Perspectives* (co-editor, 1991).

List of abbreviations

APU	Assessment and Performance Unit
AWPU	age-weighted pupil unit
CAO	Chief Administrative Officer
CDT	craft, design and technology
CEC	Community Education Council
CIPFA	Chartered Institute of Public Finance and Accountancy
CSG	Curriculum Study Group
CTC	City Technology College
DES	Department of Education and Science
DFE	Department for Education
FAS	Funding Agency for Schools
FE	further education
GEST	Grants for Education Support and Training
GLC	Greater London Council
GM	grant-maintained
GTC	General Teaching Council
HE	higher education
HMI	Her Majesty's Inspectorate
IIP	'Investors in People'
ILEA	Inner London Education Authority
ITT	initial teacher-training
LCC	London County Council
LEA	local education authority
LMS	local management of schools
OECD	Organization for Economic Co-operation and Development
OFSTED	Office for Standards in Education
PTA	parent–teacher association
SCAA	School Curriculum and Assessment Authority
SHA	Secondary Heads Association
SRE	standard resource unit
SSA	standard spending assessment

TGAT   Task Group on Assessment and Testing
TEC   Training and Enterprise Council
TU   trade union
TVEI   Technical and Vocational Education Initiative

PART I

Changing relationships and authority frameworks

CHAPTER 1

The context of development

VIVIAN WILLIAMS

In this first chapter the main strands in the development towards self-managing schools are traced from the mid-1960s to the sweeping reforms of the 1988 and 1993 Education Acts. The review focuses broadly on developments relevant to issues covered by other contributors to this book. Regretfully, several substantial thrusts in government strategies have been omitted – not least being consideration of the impact of reform on teaching as a professional occupation; dissent over curriculum reform and pupil assessment; difficulties over changing roles and increasing technical specialization required of headteachers and their colleagues, parents and governing bodies of schools in undertaking their new responsibilities.

As a teacher and former senior LEA officer, the writer believes the loss of shared responsibility for education and dynamism in former partnerships may lead to even greater losses in traditional values and educational purpose.

Meandering with intent towards systemic change

The foundations for schooling during the past fifty years were provided in the Education Act of 1944. As in earlier years of this century, local education authorities (LEAs) were given wide duties and powers under that Act to initiate developments in the provision of improved opportunities for educational continuity from nursery to further education (Williams, 1976). During the next two decades, significant and distinctive features of post-war development were characterized by the application of the principle of consensual and gradualist educational policies mediated through partnerships between central government, LEAs and teachers' associations to achieve national and local development (Kogan, 1971).

In this country as elsewhere, education systems respond to significant socio-economic trends and many subsequent developments have occurred – perhaps the most notable being the gradual introduction of comprehensive, non-selective secondary schools during the 1960s and 1970s. The period also marked the end of the post-war culture of educational consensus; of carefully considered and thoughtful, measured processes of change frequently following in the wake of government-commissioned reports. Many of these incremental changes have been subsequently framed within new legislation but others, such as the development of secondary comprehensive education, were accomplished through evolutionary change in the existing uncentralized system. Until the late 1960s, strategies for educational change and development were formulated, negotiated and implemented in an enduring culture of mutual regard, trust and commitment within a policy formulation troika of providers – the minister and the government department, the LEA associations and the teachers' unions (Locke, 1974).

However, during the late 1960s public unease with the education system gradually emerged as achievement of anticipated political, employer and parental expectations remained elusive and largely unrealized during a period when, somewhat paradoxically, resource provision for the physical expansion in the education service was considerable and on an unprecedented scale. Relative deprivation at economic, social and educational levels led to a variety of insistent demands for improvement as well as expansion. Systemic educational problems were addressed and serial compendious solutions proposed across the whole of the education service through influential 'progressive' reports such as Crowther, Newsom, Robbins and Plowden. Contemporaneously, critical 'reactionary' essays about the quality of education provided in schools, exemplified through the publication of collections of 'Black Papers', fuelled perceptions of relative deprivation and about the authenticity of fashionable expansion in educational 'opportunity' (Cox and Dyson, 1969). Universally confident expectations were gradually eroded and replaced by endemic uncertainty voiced among politicians, parents, employers and, for other and quite different reasons, by teachers.

Although beyond the immediate focus of this book, it should be added that many teachers, dissatisfied with the secondary school bipartite system, had enthusiastically embraced both the concept and establishment of secondary comprehensive schools. Positive considerations for the development of comprehensive schools were that they would mark the end of manifest injustice to children through flawed selection processes at 11-plus; introduce equalization of opportunities for all pupils; and promote social cohesion through new forms of pupil grouping in schools (Benn and Simon, 1972).

To carry through these radical changes, new curricula were developed for 11- to 16-year-old pupils. Alongside the established General Certificate of Education (GCE) examination at Ordinary level, and following extended gestation, a new form of school-leaving examination was introduced in 1965 – the Certificate of Secondary Education (CSE) – to stimulate new curricular programmes and methods of teaching and learning in secondary schools. Tangential to these developments, largely initiated, organized and provided in schools through LEA advisory and financial support, the government Department of Education and Science (DES) and Her Majesty's Inspectorate (HMI) attempted through a new Curriculum Study Group (CSG) to develop curriculum strategies that might both inform its own educational policy and influence practice in schools. However, and arising from concerns raised by the LEAs and teachers' associations about central government intervention in the curricula of schools, the life-span of the CSG was brief. Nevertheless, it planted the first seeds for development of a national curriculum in 'the undergrowth of education' (Mann, 1979). In 1964 the preliminary process for moving obliquely towards a strategy for national curriculum development was given formal recognition through the Schools Council for Curriculum and Examinations in an uneasily extended partnership of the DES, the LEAs and the teachers' associations (Plaskow, 1985).

The specific objectives of the Schools Council were to promote educational development through research projects into, and the practical development of, a wide range of curricular, examinations and teaching concerns – many of which were adopted and proved to be influential in shaping areas of the curriculum in schools for some two decades. Later, in 1975 the DES established the Assessment of Performance Unit (APU) to formulate ways in which curricula might be monitored and assessed at national level. Through these and other initiatives early interventionist moves into former autonomous areas of teachers in schools and encroachment upon traditional independent LEA policies for local development and control occurred.

Further signs of tentative but perceptible encroachment into the 'authority' of schools for curriculum responsibility and that of the LEAs for determining independent organizational policies appeared through clarification of legal questions of that authority under provisions of the 1944 Education Act. For example, in 1967, parents and ratepayers challenged the Enfield LEA over its proposals for the comprehensive reorganization of its schools. Further, in 1976 when the DES displayed unwarranted confidence about the extent of central government powers over LEAs (Section 68 of the 1944 Act), the Minister of Education suffered an unprecedented defeat in the courts through an action brought by the Tameside LEA (Alexander and Williams, 1978).

Nevertheless, during this period, the DES and HMI were gradually developing increasingly interventionist policies, many stemming from the establishment of the Planning Branch introduced in 1967 which was, in turn, replaced by a larger Departmental Planning Organization in 1970. Steady growth in interventionist activity was revealed in the publication of the 1972 White Paper *Education: A Framework for Expansion* which for the first time established a planning basis of national objectives for the education system. Significantly, within the context of future developments, the White Paper was produced without public consultation with either LEAs or the teachers' professional associations. In 1975, this style of concealed policy-making by the DES attracted the attention of an OECD team which appeared surprised to find that there were no 'formal institutions of consultation requiring officers of the Department regularly to exchange views with the various constituencies affected by their plan or to defend their decision against criticism' (Organization for Economic Co-operation and Development, 1975). It appears that central government departmental strategy has continued in an undeviating direction in spite of subsequent scrutiny of educational policies and performance undertaken by several parliamentary sub-committees (Lawrence, 1992).

As already noted, confidence in both purpose and performance in the education system was declining and, redolent of the fictional 'Yes Prime Minister' reactive style, both the DES and HMI were reorganized. For example, in 1977 a significant reorganization of HMI occurred through the policy of First Call Centre duties (Pile, 1979). Under this partial refashioning of purpose and role, up to 25 per cent of HMIs were allocated to work on national education surveys and specific studies for extended periods with the objective of providing data for the DES to advise on the formulation of future government education policy. This DES strategy to extend its power and influence was evident in its 1976 brief on the education system for the new Prime Minister, James Callaghan. The Department produced a confidential, but widely leaked, report on the education system and the highly critical tenor of the document provided the basis of the Prime Minister's Oxford speech in late 1976 (*The Times Educational Supplement*, October 1976).

The assertion by some commentators that the temporal boundary demarcating the end of earlier policy consensus and mutuality of interests in educational development came through the intervention of James Callaghan is not entirely accurate (Bash and Coulby, 1989). Rather, Callaghan's intervention was a public acknowledgement of the end of a phase when the steadily crumbling consensual partnership finally collapsed. His intervention signalled an intention of directly explicit central government intervention into education which has intensified throughout the past seventeen years. It indicated that a fundamental rubicon had been crossed and that the spirit of, and conventions established following, the Education Act of 1944 were to be set aside. Taylor and Saunders (1976) provide a useful contemporary perspective on the gradual shift in power relationships during the thirty years following the Act:

> It is true that ... extensive ministerial powers have been sparingly used though recourse to this section [Education Act, 1944, Section 1] by the Secretary of State has been more frequent in the current decade, but the powers ... to issue regulations [statutory instruments] have proved an effective way of exercising detailed control over local authorities.
>
> (p. 4)

In addition to increasingly detailed central government control over LEAs, the continuation of power-shifts towards central government has been widened and accelerated through subsequent legislation with an unprecedented assumption of ministerial authority over the control and direction of education policy. Thus, the Education Act 1988 was considered by Maclure (1989) as 'the most important and far-reaching piece of educational law-making . . . since the Education Act of 1944'.

Public accountability: launch-pad for reform

In 1976, through his policy speech and 'great debate' on education, Callaghan voiced at the highest political level rising public unease over the system's perceived failure to deliver the considerable expectations anticipated following unprecedented expansion of educational provision. Virtually all of these expectations were predicated on assumptions about 'education' as investment in the construction of the highway to a more egalitarian and economically successful society. However, by 1976, and as outlined above, a retreat from the confident educational expansion of earlier years was clearly evident; not least over claims about declining educational and social standards in secondary comprehensive schools, intensified by deteriorating national economic conditions and marked demographic decline.

Contrastingly, the retreat coincided with rapidly increasing levels of public expenditure – much of it attributed to an expensive and ill-judged restructuring of local government in 1974. Within the newly enlarged LEAs mounting public concern over more remote and increasingly unresponsive, bureaucratized local government systems became increasingly focused on a failure to articulate clearly the objectives and outcomes of the public education system. For many parents, schools were disarmingly encouraging about the progress of individual pupils who subsequently failed to achieve desired parental goals when measured against requirements for entry to higher education or to secure 'white collar' jobs.

These concerns were steadily fuelled through high-octane media output providing adverse publicity about falling achievement standards, rising behavioural problems during adolescence and curricula lacking coherence, purpose and direction. Stimulated, if not invoked, by BBC programmes such as *Panorama* about comprehensive schools; school 'culture', as portrayed in the BBC's *Grange Hill*; the ILEA enquiry into the problems at Risinghill and, later, at the William Tyndale School, all amplified by 'revelations' in the tabloid press – mounting social concern led to political pressure within both of the major political parties for the introduction of some form of educational accountability (Gretton and Jackson, 1976). 'Progressive' teachers, researchers, teacher-trainers, teachers' unions and LEAs were all derided at various times during the mid- to late 1970s in rising criticisms over educational purpose, process and outcomes in schools, colleges and universities.

In his 1976 Oxford speech, Callaghan avoided use of the term 'accountability' but his intentions were explicit and the text was released in advance to ensure full media attention. His determination to reflect and align with public perceptions of serious shortcomings in the education system was uncompromising:

It is as though some people would wish that the subject matter and purpose of education should not have public attention focused on it; or at any rate that profane hands should not be allowed to touch it. . . . Public interest is strong and will be satisfied. It is legitimate . . . so there will be discussion. . . . I repeat that parents, teachers, learned and professional bodies, representatives of higher education and both sides of industry, together with the Government, all have an important part to play in formulating and expressing the purpose of education and the standards we need. . . . To the teachers I would say that you must satisfy parents and industry that what you are doing meets their requirements and the needs of their children. If the public is not convinced then the profession will be laying up trouble for itself in the future. It will be an advantage to the teaching profession to have a wide public understanding and support for what they are doing.

(*Education*, 22 October 1976, pp. 332–3)

Callaghan's call for public discussion was organized through a series of regional conferences and subsequently crystallized in a government Green Paper in 1977. Now the term 'accountability' was used. Some of Callaghan's points were unveiled in the Green Paper through trenchant criticism of existing general educational practice in schools. Four themes were identified for critical public discussion: curricula; standards and assessment; schools in relation to occupational life and the community; initial and post-experience training of teachers. All four themes have continued as recurrent and major foci for policy initiatives and legislative reform during the past decade.

In curriculum development in schools, for example, a review of LEA provision was required by the DES, following which *A Framework for the Curriculum* was published and then an HMI publication, *A View of the Curriculum*, both in 1980. Both documents provided clear signals of central government expectations over curriculum provision in schools. In 1981, a further publication from HMI, *The School Curriculum*, was followed by a stream of documents on curriculum matters in harness with various DES circulars requiring implementation by LEAs. It was claimed that in the decade between 1976 and 1986 the combined DES/HMI output on curriculum matters exceeded the entire published output from central government on the curriculum during the previous century (Brighouse, 1986).

The extract from the Callaghan speech repays careful perusal. Not only did it illustrate the nature of widespread public and DES concerns during the mid-1970s but it foreshadowed some of the major policies for fundamental change in the 1988 Education Act. It is open to question whether clairvoyance was among Callaghan's many political skills but, and more importantly, it revealed an abiding strategy at the DES. Callaghan proved to be the political herald for ways in which educational concerns were to become subsequently extrapolated as radically reformist educational policies by successor governments. However, in 1976, Callaghan pressed for a different solution based on more consciously shared partnerships between 'producers' and 'consumers' to generate greater awareness among stakeholders about educational purpose, mutuality, trust and understanding of their legitimate roles. In doing so, he was also foreshadowing future power-shifts within the partnership – from 'providers' to 'clients' and an awareness of a presumed legitimacy of 'market interests'. Further, publication of the Taylor Report in 1977 and its radical recommendations for a depoliticized, professional-community framework of school governance broke the ground for the local management of schools a decade later.

During the final two years of the Callaghan government, and arising from subsequent public debate, various funded research projects examined concepts and models of educational accountability. Product and, especially, process evaluation models and procedures were adopted in many LEAs leading to a general acceptance within the 'educational establishment' of the inevitability of the introduction of forms of educational accountability to new constituencies and stakeholders – notably, parents and employers – perceived as the main client groups. However, change occurred only in small incremental steps and at glacial pace. Before any significant assessment of the implementation of the Callaghan/Shirley Williams policy initiatives could be undertaken or any systemic reform introduced, the Labour government lost office in 1979 to be replaced by a Conservative government, led (if that is not too acerbic a verb) by Margaret Thatcher. At the time of writing, various versions of Conservative governments, currently with John Major as Prime Minister, have held office continuously since 1979.

Templates for systemic reform

Almost immediately, the Thatcher government set about the tasks of educational reform which reflected some of the salient concerns of the Callaghan government between 1976 and 1979. The thrust of government reformist strategies was, thus, unbroken although the nostrums for educational 'improvement' now came from radically different political ideologies. Simultaneously, further curtailment of public sector expenditure became an immediate government policy priority on the assumption of office and has been sustained without amelioration. With a numerical decline in total school population and the generally perceived failure of existing education provision as a mainspring for technological change and success, public sector education budgets were immediately susceptible to retrenchment policies and systemic reform. The ascendancy of politically influential 'New Right' education paradigms hastened and legitimized the tranche of subsequent reforms (Bondi, 1991).

During the first few years of determined central government interventionist strategies, the forensic style of Sir Keith Joseph, the longest-serving Secretary of State for Education during Conservative administration, was publicly evident. From 1981 to 1986, he launched a raft of centralizing policies for the reform of the system with a 'market rationale' and objectives for specific change. Innovative policies included the introduction of a vocational strand in secondary school curricula through the introduction of the Technical and Vocational Education Initiative (TVEI); direct intervention in the initial and post-experience training of teachers; and, most significantly, had oversight of radical new policies for a reformed curriculum and its delivery in schools. The government's declared policy objectives were to raise standards for all levels of ability in schools and to secure efficient and effective returns on resources provided for education. Strategies to secure these objectives moved in two broad directions: education that was relevant and appropriate to achieve national policies and a determination to secure implementation of those policies in explicit centrally controlled ways.

In relation to these policies, a White Paper, *Teaching Quality* (1983), acknowledged that teachers were 'the major single determinant of the quality of education' and then argued that to make effective use of the teaching force accurate knowledge of teacher performance was required and should be derived from assessment of individual practitioners involving 'classroom visiting by the teacher's head or head of department and an appraisal of both pupils' work and the teacher's contribution to the life of the school'. In 1985, a further government White Paper, *Better Schools*, extended the concept of performance appraisal to include systematic and effective support and development through the deployment of staff more effectively 'by developing their strengths and improving upon their weaknesses' and providing the key instrument for improved management of relationships between 'pay, responsibilities and performance, especially teaching performance in the classroom'. This was also a period of intensive publication of HMI papers such as *Slow Learners and Less Successful Pupils in Secondary Schools* (1984), and *The Curriculum from 5 to 16* and *Quality in Schools: Evaluation and Appraisal* – both during 1985 (Williams, 1985).

As exemplified in the preceding paragraph, successive DES and HMI publications, government White Papers and Education Acts (for example, those of 1980, 1981, 1986, 1988, 1992 and 1993) together with new Statutory Regulations introduced policies that have sought, at least ostensibly, to raise standards in schools at all ability levels; to introduce consistency in curriculum entitlement for pupils and phased national assessment; and to devise cross-curricular studies perceived as relevant to social and, especially, economic development. During the decade of the 1980s efficient and effective returns on public sector resources invested in the education system were demanded and governmental measures to secure demonstrable and public accountability from teachers and schools were vigorously pursued, e.g. legislation for the performance appraisal of teachers was introduced in the 1986 Act and a National Curriculum mandated in the 1988 Act. A review of inherent school self-management issues involved in the performance appraisal of teachers is provided by Ed McConnell in Chapter 6.

The 1988 Education Act was intended to consolidate earlier piecemeal legislative changes during the early 1980s and to create a radically new education system. Government intentions were clearly signalled in a 1987 parliamentary speech by Kenneth Baker, then Secretary of State for Education: 'we need to inject new vitality into the system. It has become producer-dominated' – an echo of the Callaghan criticisms a decade earlier.

Government policy was profoundly influenced by politically fashionable trends of the 1980s for market ideologies, individual consumerism and government determination to eliminate distinctions between public and private sector organizations. Importantly, government solutions were designed to increase parental choice and institutional diversity in education provision. As was considered politically attractive, the government regarded parents as both consumers of, and decision-makers to secure, improved educational opportunities. Traditional powers of LEAs represented a major stumbling-block to this policy and were largely removed through provisions in the 1988 Education Act. The Act reflected government determination finally to remove the monolithic control exercised by LEAs for public sector educational provision within their areas. An explicit policy for altering the balance between provider and client interests in favour of the latter was introduced through legal transference of most LEA duties, powers and responsibilities directly to schools and their governing bodies. In addition, responsibilities for curriculum content, development and control were removed from LEA control and assumed by central government as was stewardship for the assessment of national attainment standards.

The LEAs

The pivotal over-arching strategy has been to remove virtually all the legal powers of LEAs for schools and their control of educational provision. Consequently, discretionary powers of local authorities for the distribution of central government financial allocations to schools were also withdrawn. The significance of political and financial weakening of LEAs may be gauged from a realization that the education budgets of LEAs were larger than the aggregated totals of all other local authority services. Thus, devolution of financial and personnel functions to individual governing bodies of most schools – claimed to be more representative of community and parental interests – were political keystones in the 1988 reforms and were achieved through the introduction of local management of schools (LMS).

Earlier in the 1980s, policies for extension of school autonomy and client choice had been introduced through the 'assisted places' scheme and followed by the creation of an autonomous cluster of City Technology Colleges (CTC) (Whitty et al., 1993). But these innovative strategies intended to broaden opportunities for parental choice and educational diversity were seen as small-scale developments, albeit politically important ones, when compared with the creation of an entirely new sector of publicly funded self-managing schools under the 1988 Education Act. Above all other reforms, the new sector of grant-maintained (GM) schools characterized the application of client-focused policies and represented the determination of the government to dismantle the LEA framework as a tier in the governance, control and provision of the education service. Sustained government campaigns of negative criticism of LEAs as unco-operative, politically subjective and non-accountable decision-making bureaucracies, and as inefficient resource allocators diverting central government funding for education into other municipal projects, were used to justify sweeping reform of the existing education system.

In this climate of the politics of derogation, cynically inclined observers detected the emergence of adventitious political stratagems following the government's election to office in 1979. As a result of acrimonious confrontations between the government and several Labour-controlled and predominantly urban LEAs over its new education policies and associated expenditure controls during the early 1980s, it was inevitable that the former would adopt a more confrontational stance. The mechanisms of the assisted places scheme, the formula for partnerships between central government and business interests to establish CTCs, the creation of an entirely new category of GM schools directly responsible to the DES (reorganized as the Department for Education (DFE) in 1992) together with the introduction of LMS all reflected ways in which LEAs were removed from the educational 'high ground'.

Under the 1993 Education Act, that process has been taken further. A new Funding Agency for Schools (FAS) is to be established with, *inter alia*, responsibilities for the funding of GM schools. Where there is an enrolment of between 10 and 75 per cent of pupils at GM schools in an LEA area, responsibility for planning provision of an adequate number of school places will be shared between the FAS and the LEA. Where the GM school enrolment exceeds 75 per cent of pupils, the FAS will supersede the LEA as the planning body for ensuring adequate numbers of school places are available. At the time of writing it is anticipated that at least 50 per cent of all LEAs will be required to share their former forward planning responsibilities with the FAS.

Local management of schools (LMS)

Whatever reservation existed over some government policies, the concept of LMS appeared to be both a logical and a desirable innovation in the 1988 Education Act. To devolve power and responsibility for decision-making to local community and school-site level through the earlier reconstructed school governing bodies was regarded as an appropriate and justified extension of the principle of parents and teachers as the major stakeholders. Ironically, development projects for increased self-management through successful delegation of budgetary control to schools initiated by some LEAs (notably in Cambridgeshire and Solihull) had been actively supported by governing bodies and headteachers. Unsurprisingly, government policies for greater financial autonomy in schools through systemic change were welcomed especially by schools and governing bodies. Further, it was believed that LMS would overcome widely publicized criticisms of LEAs as cumbersome self-regarding local bureaucracies with stifling effects on educational initiative, enterprise, efficiency and effectiveness of schools.

In addition, and perhaps fortuitous in its timing, evidence in support of the development of successful site-based self-managing school systems came from overseas. Experience gained from projects in Australia and Canada suggested that policies leading to the development of self-managing schools offered solutions to many of the problems inhibiting educationally effective and financially efficient management of schools (Caldwell and Spinks, 1988).

For England and Wales, government strategy for its centralizing reforms was in anticipation of compliance by individual school governing bodies in respect of their new local responsibilities. Under central government prescriptions, governing bodies have been given responsibility for the implementation of the centrally prescribed National Curriculum and its associated assessment regime through local deployment of the new formula-driven site-specific budgets, and presumed cost-benefits, at school level. In Chapter 4, John Howells provides a review of the radical changes involved in creating the mechanisms required for the successful introduction of LMS in a self-managing school geared both to efficiency and effectiveness in the discharge of its many responsibilities to pupils, parents and community. From a general perspective it has to be accepted that there has been a loss of the broadly focused binocular overview and expertise of LEA continuity and vigilance for educational provision in their geographical areas which is being replaced by more closely focused monocular perceptions of educational priorities within individual school and local community considerations.

As illustrated by John Howells in Part II of this book, under the umbrella of LMS mechanisms government policies have established a framework of self-managing schools with governing bodies responsible for the more effective use of allocated finances to achieve national objectives – principally in the deployment of resources to deliver requirements of the National Curriculum and assessment of pupil progress. Through flexibility offered by budgetary virement, schools are able to prioritize finances to achieve national objectives and are given freedom to pursue locally determined ones. At both national and local levels it is intended that schools will become more responsive to local client groups: parents, community and employers. The accountability of schools and individual teachers is also an explicit objective in relation to achievement of stipulated national and local priorities.

However, individual schools might also become narrowly parochial through limited ambition and bounded opportunities for their pupils. This possibility may perhaps be an unsought, unintended outcome of planned increased central government control but for many parents and teachers it is a real and an unwelcome one. Some commentators believe that the notion of 'power to the people', in this instance parents and local communities, is largely illusory and less important than the government's undeviating determination to tighten its grasp on the education system through wrenching the steering reins of educational development – the curriculum, assessment and public sector expenditure – from LEA control (Bash and Coulby, 1989).

To facilitate that tightened steering control, the powers of LEA have been extensively reduced and their former direct responsibilities for local schools effectively withdrawn. Currently, further weakening of LEA responsibility is occurring. LEAs retain some residual tasks including the disbursing of central government grant allocations to schools in accordance with schemes of financial delegation submitted to, and approved by, the DFE. Through a curiously clumsy mechanism, LEAs retain formal responsibility for the appointment and dismissal of teachers although in practice such decisions are effectively under the control of governing bodies. Independent and discretionary financial decision-making by LEAs has been largely removed other than for a limited number of collectively provided services for which LEAs may, or must continue to, retain responsibility for maintained schools in their geographical areas. Residual LEA services include responsibilities for and arrangement of school attendance, transportation to and from school, psychological assessment of pupils, adequate provision for pupils with special needs, arrangements for school milk and meals in necessitous cases, the careers service, health and safety requirements, standards of premises, capital expenditure programmes and hypothecated grant-funding and awards to students in higher education. An important retained duty of the LEAs is to monitor and evaluate the devolved LMS arrangements within a framework of approved performance indicators. In their contributions to this book, David Church and David Hill explore existing and possible future LEA roles in the reformed system. Eventually, it is anticipated that more than 90 per cent of government funding allocations for schools will be delegated to schools, and LEAs, if they continue to exist, will become merely agents of central government.

Government policies to remove former substantial powers of LEAs were most clearly evident within the new framework of LMS. Following legislation in 1988, each LEA was required to submit to the DES a scheme for the delegation of self-managing powers to its schools in preparation for the introduction of LMS. With the introduction of LMS, LEAs have applied approved government formulae to calculate the distribution of central funding to individual schools. Formula allocations are calculated on many variables, the most important being a capitation component. This is an age-weighted pupil unit (AWPU) formula which is applied across the age range of enrolled pupils attending each school. Of the total of centrally provided resources allocated through the AWPU formula a minimum of 75 per cent of individual school allocated budgets is derived from this single source. Other elements in the formulae for delegated budgets to schools include recognition by LEAs of historic funding elements such as the age and condition of school buildings, the number of pupils with designated special educational needs, assessment of variables such as poverty, linguistic and ethnic criteria. However, as the range of LEA discretionary services might reduce the totals of direct allocation of funds to schools, the government placed an upper limit on LEA central office retention with the requirement that such retention would taper to less than 10 per cent of centrally provided funding.

Within these policy constraints, LEAs have applied to all primary, special and secondary schools the prescribed formulae predicated on inexact assumptions that equitable standards of provision could be achieved (DES, 1988). Clearly, this was, and is, an unrealistic objective as schools vary considerably in age, size, condition, equipment, pupils' differentiated needs and teaching staff biographical profiles. For example, smaller schools require larger, enhanced capitation allowances than those for larger schools – this is especially noticeable in relation to the curriculum entitlement model adopted for delivery of the prescribed National Curriculum and the provision for special needs provision within and beyond the 'statementing' requirement. In Chapter 5, Michael Fossey outlines the problems and solutions in one LEA in relation to formula funding, especially over making provision for pupils with special educational needs.

In addition to those considerations and central to the problematical National Curriculum educational model for schools, a major difficulty exists over the determination of the teaching establishment of schools. Within broad tolerances over effective and efficient provision of education every school is at liberty to establish and employ a self-determined complement of teachers – both in terms of total size and local emphases over the achievement of curricular and social objectives. However, under the formula-driven funding calculations, the DFE has assumed an 'average teacher' salary formula rather than 'actual' staffing costs. As a generalized approximation, 75 to 80 per cent of delegated school budgets are required for teachers' salaries and serious problems have arisen in the staffing of schools. For example, many governing bodies and headteachers have been required to make unpalatable choices when replacing older, experienced and, thus, more expensive teachers with successors who are younger, inexperienced but relatively inexpensive. Because of financial constraints, selection criteria may become unprecedentedly skewed towards non-educational considerations – and some difficult decisions are required when appointing staff in schools. These are matters of considerable concern for school governing bodies and headteachers. Examples of such myopic considerations are not uncommon in correspondence published in weekly educational journals (*Times Educational Supplement*, 1992).

'Opting out': the grant-maintained sector of schools (GM)

Another thrust in the government's determination to end the earlier dominant role of LEAs and initiate corporate parental choice within the maintained system of public education was provided in the 1988 Act and reinforced by the 1993 Education Act. A substantial section of the 1988 Act provided for an unprecedented opting-out procedure for schools within LEAs to create a new category of self-managing GM schools directly financed by central government. From inception, GM schools have received larger recurrent and capital financial allocations than schools remaining within the LEA sector. Although delegation of control to maintained schools under LMS attracted widespread approval, the creation of an autonomous GM category of maintained and it will become an irreversibly established school category because of the presumed degree of community/parental support for the sector and anticipated public antipathy over any proposal for the reintroduction of an LEA framework (Chubb and Moe, 1992).

Parental choice: issues of 'exit' and 'voice'

The political nostrums of 'school autonomy' and 'consumer choice' have been extended to other systemic educational functions. Concern is growing that through the application of local school 'autonomy' and parental 'choice', social equity and open access to educational provision are at risk and may be replaced by concepts of selection and elitism in many schools. For example, and in addition to developments outlined earlier in this chapter, the possible expansion of the voluntary aided school sector under the 1993 Act may lead to extensive partitioned education provision firmly under strategic policy and financial controls of central government – whatever its political persuasion – and the potential danger of the liberality of earlier freedom of access to educational opportunities and concepts of social and cultural diversity in educational processes being subordinated to predominantly economic considerations.

It is these concerns together with the loss of local democratic accountability and organizational unity following the planned removal of LEAs as major mediators of educational policy and development that have led to major reservations about government policies during the past five or so years. For some, the longitudinally measured policy perspectives of LEAs are being replaced by short-term political consumerism and subjective priorities of many articulate parents. Education is manifestly not a free-market zone as the vast majority of schools, providing education for some 90 per cent of pupils between the ages of 5 and 18 years, are funded from government public sector allocations and under central control. Unless parents are able to afford significantly high fees for their children to attend independent schools, 'choice' is largely confined to maintained schools that are required to accept centrally prescribed curricular and financial objectives.

Even within a state-controlled and funded system there are issues of autonomy and choice which have become sharper both in terms of focus and in terms of effect following the introduction of local management of schools and the creation of the GM schools sector. Through its policies and subsequent legislation for reform the government assembled a politically attractive package, ostensibly to provide greater opportunities for parental responsibility and diversity. Direct control over educational provision and finance has been achieved via the exercise of 'constrained choice' through limited devolved powers for the curriculum and prescribed financial formulae under central government control in the local management of schools.

Nevertheless, it is important to recall that prior to the 1988 Education Act, parents were not considered as powerful stakeholders in educational provision in the public sector. Although Section 76 of the 1944 Education Act conferred a degree of parental choice it was heavily circumscribed through unilateral interpretation by LEAs of their duties and powers. Formal parental complaints about academic, social and resource provision of education in schools could be made to the school governing body, the LEA and, as a last resort, to the then DES which tended to support decisions taken by LEAs. Further, requests for transfer of pupils to alternative schools were granted only when resource implications were unproblematic and permission to move out of defined catchment areas was secured from the LEA. Thus, unless parents were articulate, knowledgeable, persuasive and persistent, their 'voice' was generally subdued and ineffective. Overwhelmingly, 'exit' choice was available only to those who could afford to pay fees at independent schools.

Undeniably, the government's determination to 'carry the concept of parental choice to the heart of our educational system . . . to move the balance of discretionary power away from providers of education to its clients' (*Hansard*, House of Commons, 20 November 1987. The Secretary of State's statement on the Education Reform Bill in the House of Commons) was explicit in the legislation over reforms for LMS and GM schools in the 1988 Act. In the view of Kenneth Baker, then Secretary of State for Education:

> If the product is not all that it should be, parents should not be put in a position of having to like it or lump it. Grant-maintained schools will be a threat to the complacent and to the second best. They will also challenge all within the service to do better. . . . Their [GM schools'] success will depend upon their management and upon parental commitment and that recipe, through financial delegation and more open enrolment, is available to all schools. . . . I want to give people a chance to press for excellence; I want to give them the means to demand excellence; and I want to create a spur which will oblige all LEAs to deliver excellence.
>
> (Sayer and Williams, 1989, p. 149)

Accordingly, since 1988 central government reformist policies for local governance and management of schools have provided parents with new opportunities for, but also dilemmas over, choice. Following the introduction of the Parent's Charter in 1991 and the new statutory requirements of the 1988 Education Act, information is available to parents on relative attainment levels achieved by schools through the publication of educational performance tables based on unrefined public examination and standardized test outcomes, pupil attendance/truancy ratios, destinations of school-leavers and via summaries of external school inspection reports on planned four-year cycles. Examples of parental dilemmas may be summarized as choices now between 'exit' to another state-funded school (under existing open-enrolment policies) or, as in earlier years, 'exit' to an independent school if parents can afford to pay the required fees. Alternatively, and perhaps as parent-governors or through membership of parent-teacher associations, parents can adopt an active partnership 'voice' role through seeking to find remedies for perceived dissatisfaction with neighbourhood schools. With unprecedented access to information about local schools, it is argued that parents are now able to make inscription of unprecedented powers leading to a centralized education system controlled under a carapace of legislative, prescriptive and financial autocracy warrants public opprobrium.

Specifically, since the 1988 Act, an avalanche of mandated structural change has sought pragmatically to focus on 'efficient' education provision and has largely ignored questions of 'effective' educational purpose and earlier enduring values at individual and collective scales. Change in education is both normal and inevitable but successful change occurs only when those involved in contributing to the process are included in policy formulation, planning and implementation of development. During the past five years, substantial problems have arisen in education reform principally not because of the policies that have been pursued but through the absence of sustained discourse with those who have been required to implement them.

The education service of England and Wales requires positive, progressively challenging development through 'open' government policies together with professional and community support at legislative and operational levels. Among consistent governmental oversights in recent years, perhaps the most regrettable and damaging has been the failure to acknowledge and adequately support an obvious educational truism that it is at individual school level that policy prescriptions, mandated curricular innovation and budgetary priorities are implemented. It is those teachers and administrators directly employed in schools and LEAs who have to interpret and deliver policy-in-action programmes and through their professional commitment strive to provide *educational opportunities for all pupils* within the corsetry of legislated provision for *schooling*. The central and local tasks involved are of entirely different qualitative dimensions – a fundamental insight missing from virtually all activitin in recent government reform.

During the past five years the cutting edge of that reform has been honed on the whetstone of ideologically driven political considerations – for curricular and management policies. The impact of all prescribed national policies has its greatest effects on pupils and teachers in schools and it is there that the realities of insight and genuine understanding of values such as 'citizenship', 'access', 'equity' and 'education as investment' are practicably perceived, sharply experienced and reality-tested. It is these values which provide the real yardsticks for educational opportunities in contrast to the more limited vision of schooling. They also provide the source for educational objectives that are realizable only through perceptions of ownership in self-motivated commitment by teachers to their pupils. If teachers and pupils are to achieve these objectives, the work of schools requires the active participation of and support from parents, local communities and central government. These, not merely structural considerations, are the real issues in educational reform. They were glimpsed in new partnership proposals during the 'great debate' of 1976—77 but, although now more urgent, have received short shrift in recent years in central government policies.

These values have been further jeopardized through the wholesale and rapid dismantling of an educational system that evolved gradually and thoughtfully during the past century being replaced by a hurriedly reformed system that emphasizes outcomes which are amenable to statistical calculation or measured through apparently mechanistic periodic school inspections. Educational objectives that hitherto have been valued in our educational system, and are largely intangible, lifelong, cultural, ethical and spiritual, but not susceptible to quantitative measurement, are currently at risk of permanent removal from the life and work of schools. It is to be hoped that further legislation and, above all, consultation with representative groups of those who daily provide educational opportunities for pupils will redirect the existing politically inspired reformist zeal towards positive gains in the continuity of national achievement, humanity and culture. If the present trend continues a new tradition will emerge in a reformed system leading to outcomes of irretrievable individual and community loss through immutable educational values being supplanted by material philistinism. We will know precisely the cost of everything and the value of nothing in our educational system.

Recent history of legislated educational change suggests that the exercise of unilateral central government political self-interest is a fundamentally flawed strategy to achieve effective reform. It is self-evident that the charting of new pathways towards educational improvement is both overdue and urgent. However, the present direction of systemic change is moving away from much that is central and valued in our educational tradition and culture. With the introduction of organizationally vulnerable self-managing schools there is, in the opinion of the writer, a considerable risk of the emergence of a fragmented, partitioned education system predicated on questionable assumptions about the benefits of short-term material considerations. If this were to occur, a greater threat will emerge – that of undemocratic, insensitive and centrally controlled unaccountable bureaucracies in which issues of choice and freedom will, yet again, continue to be available only to privileged members of a socially divisive society. For the sake of their future well-being and that of society, pupils should not be educated in a system divided against itself.

CHAPTER 2

Local education authorities: the future – what future? A personal view

DAVID CHURCH

Following many years as a teacher, a local education authority (LEA) education officer and as a senior adviser, David Church regrets the passing of the strategic educational role of LEAs – for coherent planning and provision in the development of schools and for the enhanced professionalism of teachers. He suggests possible new functions for LEAs both in the provision of services to schools within a consumer-orientated society and, especially, for the stewardship of values of entitlement and democratic accountability at individual and collective levels.

LEAs – the future – what future?

In his introductory overview Vivian Williams has graphically described the processes of gradual attrition of the powers of LEAs, followed by the seismic changes to their roles brought about through the Education Reform Act of 1988. These processes bring us to the present government's final haul towards the intended consumer-led, self-centred individual school and pupil focused, outcome for the 1990s. The 1993 Education Act is intended to bring to legislative climax the reforms that have been instituted thus far, so as to make parents the arbiters of whether or not a school succeeds in surviving, and thus to encourage schools to compete with each other for a continuing role in serving their communities. Apart from a narrow range of support functions for individual pupils, the LEA is expected to be written out of the scenario within the foreseeable future.

An historical process

In one sense, an overall interpretation of the legislative changes that have been enforced since the 1980 Education Act would put them in the historical perspective of what has happened to many of our public services in the previous 150 years or so. Many were originally commenced in response to what had been unacceptable paucity or lack of provision for the population at large – such as clean water, sewage disposal, police services and health. The private sector had often been observed to be too self-interested to use its enterprise to make provision where no profit motive existed; and too parochial in not considering the needs of wider communities or those who could not afford the service – for example, in the provision of fire services, gas and electricity and, eventually, a national system of schools.

These services were required, by government legislation largely in the nine-teenth and early part of the twentieth centuries, to be established by new public authorities, often comprising elected councillors of local authorities but sometimes through the means of single-purpose boards. When one exam-ines that list of public utilities from the perspective of 1993, one can see that one by one many have been transformed into either profit-making private enterprise companies (water, electricity, gas) or (perhaps as an interim stage) into what Bob Morris has termed 'the new magistracies' of largely unelected members attempting to exercise some gubernatorial or even managerial direc-tion over the work of the enterprise (Morris, 1990).

One could argue, therefore, that the changes in the education service are part of that general societal development – from unorganized and dislocated private enterprise, through popular legal entitlement established by local boards or local authorities and in recent years into privatized provision, re-sponsible to the shareholders in the one case and to largely non-elected governing bodies or management boards in the other. Recent political dis-cussion assumes that the police service will be next to be affected by the reduction of local accountability and its transference largely to appointed members.

There is one interesting exception to this process in the provision of per-sonal social services, which is currently being greatly extended through the closure of many hospitals/residential homes currently run by the government's health department and with the local authority social services departments being required to ensure that care for the discharged patients is provided in the local community. There may well be an analogy here with children who are physically or mentally disadvantaged or have some form of sensory deprivation and who will need champions for their rights to an appropriate education – a role perhaps for the emasculated LEAs.

What LEAs should now do

No one can argue against the fact that current and medium-term legislation will result in spending decisions and therefore power resting with the school, whether it has GM status or not. It is inconceivable that a change of political control at central government level would result in a withdrawal of the delegation of most funds to schools. There are several interesting questions for LEAs which follow from this:

- Will LEAs be permitted to continue to offer services to their schools (and, at the margin of their budgets, to other LEAs' schools and independent schools)? The prognosis is not favourable. The government intends to limit LEAs to providing services to their former schools which have become grant maintained to a maximum period of two years. After that, the government expects a competitive market to have emerged and for this to take over the provision of services.
- Will LEA teams be permitted to continue to bid for inspection contracts scheduled by the Office for Standards in Education (OFSTED)?

    Given the immutable government drive to create a competitive market, it seems that such bids for inspection work will be allowed for only so long as private companies do not exist in sufficient numbers to cover the work. As things stand at present, LEA teams that enter the competition will do so at a major disadvantage, since their full costs of doing so will inevitably be higher than those of teams comprising members who have other sources of income (especially recently redundant HMIs) or who will often be trading whilst earning their keep through other mainstream activities.
- Even more interesting, will LEA teams and their LEAs want to compete for such work?

    Small LEAs already have (for financial reasons) a problem in employing staff with sufficient expertise to cover the required curriculum for inspection purposes. Some are combining their manpower within a group of LEAs to run effective teams, but given the eventual government imperative of privatization, even this is likely to be a short-term solution. Why should LEAs wish to continue to host activities that are not a part of their brief for local services?

    LEAs, perceiving the customer/supplier relationship between their schools and themselves (and the consequent need to sustain good relationships), may also feel that it would be unwise to become involved in inspection work on behalf of OFSTED and to risk damaging their relationships with their schools in the process. Indeed, the whole new process of privatized school inspection may collapse within a very few years, on account of the failure of a market to emerge. The radical political right may well welcome this, since inspection could then be visited upon only those schools where other measures now in train – such as the publication of examination results, the publication of examination league tables, pupil attendance records and so on – fail to raise standards.

So, what's left to be done?

One starting point for this analysis is the position of the LEA *vis-à-vis* grant-maintained schools in its area. As the government press statement introducing the White Paper *Choice and Diversity: A New Framework for Schools* on 28 July 1992 stated, 'At the heart of the Government's proposals is the development of Grant Maintained Schools, both primary and secondary. On present trends, over 1,500 schools in England will be grant maintained by 1994. . . . The Government hopes that in time all schools will become Grant Maintained.' Again, the statement by Eric Forth, the junior Minister for Education, during the final debate of the committee stage of the 1993 Education Bill is interesting. He is reported as saying that GM schools would not be given the right to opt back into local government because ministers believe education authorities will not be sufficiently viable to handle them and that in most areas there would not be any authority to opt back into. The government's intentions are clear. Given that within the 1993 Education Act there will be a time-limit of two years for LEAs to continue trading with their former schools once they have become grant maintained, what will the government's ultimate solution leave the LEAs to do?

A shopping list, of course, can be constructed. It would include raising taxes to pay for a significant element (10 per cent plus) of the cost of running local services until such time as a central government can no longer bear the political fall-out of high council taxes and has sufficient margin in the national budget to accommodate the additional cost of fully funding educational expenditure centrally. The latter seems to be an unlikely imminent prospect in view of current recessionary and monetary trends. Nevertheless, government must find a solution to the dilemma that in LEAs where all, or virtually all, of one sector of schools has opted out the local authority may not wish any longer to prioritize its spending upon schools in that sector.

Secondly, between the levels of 10 per cent and 75 per cent of one sector of schools opting out, the LEA must share with a Funding Agency for Schools (FAS) the responsibility of ensuring that there are suitable and sufficient schools in its area. This strategic planning duty will be of more than passing interest to GM schools, which will need to be alive to issues arising from the building of new schools, the reorganization of existing schools and how these, and the quality of education they provide, might impact upon their educational viability

Thirdly, the LEA continues to be responsible for the creation of an agreed syllabus for religious education. Even after the 75 per cent exit point for LEA involvement in a strategic management has been reached, the LEA will continue to be responsible for ensuring that an agreed syllabus is created and reviewed, with the addition of a further conference group representing the GM sector. There is considerable potential here for LEAs to orchestrate a community view on the purposes of education and agreeing a set of values.

Fourthly, the LEA will continue to have a responsibility to ensure the regular attendance of pupils at schools and to secure admission of the pupils to either LEA or GM schools – whether under normal admission arrangements or following the creation of a statement of educational needs. LEAs will also have a duty to make educational arrangements for pupils who are no longer deemed appropriate to be educated in a maintained school. In the case of pupils with statements the LEA will, as advocated by the Audit Commission, become the purchaser of services from LEA or GM schools and will have a duty to monitor the effectiveness of the education provided by the schools (Audit Commission, 1992).

This means that LEA educational psychologists will need to know and understand the provision made in GM schools, as will the LEA special needs advisers. Presumably they can best achieve this through visiting and monitoring the work. (Further comment on the issue of the LEA as a 'customer' is made later in this chapter.)

Finally, there are the two major areas of work that still remain largely within the remit of LEAs – provision for the under-5s and community and youth education. It is possible to predict that, having lost their major influence within the schools sector, through opting out or local management of schools, local councillors will seek to develop the two services that remain within their power. Despite the current financial constraints, a few LEAs are continuing to plan and create additional facilities for under-5s. Indeed, such developments are increasingly being seen by individual councillors as a high political priority to achieve for their constituents.

It is appropriate now to return to the earlier observation concerning local authority social services functions, currently being extended to provide for people discharged into the community from residential hospitals. Clearly, where individual citizens have severe handicaps of the mind or body which limit their ability to construct a safe and secure home for themselves, the government is seeking to ensure that they are helped in doing so through support from their local authority. One can immediately identify the parallel with pupils who have special educational needs in the education system and it does not take a great stretch of the imagination to include within this group in need of support all pupils whose parents at one time or another have reason to want to query or challenge the education that the new, near-autonomous schools are providing. We have already experienced such advocacy offered by solicitors, educational psychologists and doctors in challenging statements of a pupils' special educational needs made by an LEA. Now is the time for LEAs to find ways in which they, themselves, can increasingly represent a consumer point of view. LEAs are now consumer representatives on behalf of pupils, for the quality of service provided by schools. In short, the LEA must be a guarantor of the quality of the service on behalf of people that live in the community.

As the Audit Commission (1992) recommends, LEAs should ensure a greater separation of their role with children with special educational needs from that of the schools. LEAs should adopt the role of client in a client/contractor relationship and schools as contractors should be given full responsibility for providing for the pupils. Resources should be delegated to schools and they should account for their achievements, thus allowing the LEA the opportunity to play a role as champion of children with special educational needs.

Herein, of course, rests the seed for the growth of a restructured form of local government service – the integrated education and social services department that is being created in its first materialization by the London Borough of Hillingdon. It is now clear that the role of the LEA in representing the customers of the schools is paralleled by the role of the social services department in supporting its clients. The customers/clients already overlap in their needs in many areas – the support and provision for under-5s; the educational and social needs of the 5s to 16s and the recreational, educational and social needs of the over-16s. The freedom that removal from the need to act as prime provider of services to schools now renders unto LEAs can be used to develop creative strategies for supporting individuals in their efforts to achieve satisfactory provision by the new providers. What evidence is there that communities want such a role to be played?

Where LEAs have continued to assume that they still control an empire and where their relations with their schools are characterized by harsh inspections and judgemental attitudes, then schools will carefully weigh in the balance the benefits that being part of such a structure will bring, alongside the disbenefits as they see them. On the other side of that coin, there is now evidence that in other LEAs, where principles and priorities for action are reviewed and determined in collaboration with parents, governors, teachers and elected members, then the role of the LEA in making and brokering these partnerships is greatly appreciated. Individual schools and teachers are increasingly uncomfortable with values which they see as being unforgiving to the weak and to the disadvantaged. They want the LEA to be the referee – to act and persuade from its knowledge and wide experience across many schools of how such issues can be addressed. Above all, they reject isolationism and seek collaboration and partnership in what they do. They want the LEA to create and act as guardian of a vision of a learning community; to provide leadership, establish clear standards of entitlement and accountability and to maintain a role which represents a view that is wider than that of the individual school.

Sadly, however, even the best efforts of the LEAs cannot reinstate that loss of local democratic accountability for GM schools and its transference to central government which is a product of the legislative changes. The argument that the changes mean the transfer of power not to central government but to parents and to governors is untrue. As the Association of County Councils has argued, in a democracy ultimate responsibility for a public service funded from the public purse can only be exercised by a properly elected, accountable level of government, national or local: or by the two jointly (Association of County Councils, 1993). In this sense if schools are not wholly or partly a local government responsibility exercised by LEAs, they are a national government responsibility, exercised by the Department for Education and the Funding Agency for Schools (FAS).

It is to be hoped that the exhortation to LEAs contained in this chapter will help to persuade them that even though they have lost their former power over schools they will continue to seek to influence attitudes and practice from their wider vision of what an education service might still achieve. There is much evidence that the schools, their governing bodies and their parents are willing LEAs to adopt and develop such a role. Are there leaders in the LEAs ready to do so?

CHAPTER 3

Advisory services and self-managing schools

DAVID HILL

New prescriptions for inspection, guidance and advice represent a set of problematic issues for self-managing schools. The dismantling of traditional, widely respected national and LEA services offering educational advice and guidance to schools has led to uncertainties about purpose, roles, functions and the monitoring of educational standards and development in schools. David Hill has considerable experience and expertise as a senior LEA adviser and is currently immersed in the processes of establishing new procedures for LEA services to schools required under existing central government prescriptions for 'quality control' in education. Among the processes of adjusting to new approaches, he emphasizes the crucial importance of maintaining former mutual trust and respect between colleagues in LEAs and schools in the shared pursuit of school improvement.

Inspection, advice and guidance in our schools has its origins in the early nineteenth century with the establishment of a national inspectorate whose principal role was to ensure grant aid given to certain schools was properly applied and that set standards were being achieved. In many ways, the schools themselves were 'self-managing' and worked to a curriculum code which was not too unlike a national curriculum. Changes occurred in 1870 with the establishment of school boards, and some of these established their own local 'advisory' service, designed to complement the national inspectors.

The 1902 Education Act created 315 local authorities and the several thousand school boards were subsumed within this new framework. One of the duties of these new authorities was to oversee elementary education within their boundaries. School board advisers were also absorbed within this structure and 'organizers' were appointed to develop work in music, drama and handicrafts. Following the discovery during the First World War of a population of men whose physical well-being was questionable, advisers for physical education and home economics were appointed, 50 per cent of their salaries being found by the government.

By 1918 the numbers of inspectors and advisers had grown sufficiently for an association to be formed, known as the National Association of Inspectors and Education Organizers, and this body continued to recruit additional numbers throughout the following years.

The year 1946 saw the beginnings of a slow and gradual expansion of education. Two factors were at work, an increase in birth-rate and a realization that the nation's wealth rested very firmly with the development of people, hence the growth in adult education and the raising of the school-leaving age. Further reorganization was necessary to take account of these changes. The number of local authorities was reduced (and again in 1974) and the power shift away from central government and schools towards local authority power was clearly evident. Schools now had to have local authority representatives on their governing bodies. Local authorities also took their increased responsibilities seriously enough to strengthen their schools advisory teams and, as the education authorities (LEAs) now had a monitoring role, many appointed inspectors. Examination of the growth of advisory teams in a range of LEAs suggest that the structure often lacked balance and was somewhat *ad hoc*. Northamptonshire, in 1974, illustrates the imbalance with only two primary advisers against four PE specialists, two music specialists and one specialist in each of handicraft, drama and audio-visual aids.

At the same time Her Majesty's Inspectorate (HMI) was frequently under-strength and, whilst its influence was undoubtedly high at national level, it was somewhat less at the local authority level. Often HMI came to the LEA for information on schools, on trends in schools and on difficulties schools appeared to be having. It was somewhat rare for successes to be celebrated at these meetings. Information was largely one-way from the advisory service to HMI.

Post-1974, most local authorities worked to provide a coherent team of advisers covering all subjects, cross-curricular themes and phases within their boundaries. Some authorities had worked hard to create such teams earlier than 1974, the West Riding being a prime example, where Clegg, the Chief Education Officer, had established a very powerful team. Members of this team were well-respected practitioners to whom headteachers could turn for sound advice and guidance. In many ways they held the purse-strings, especially for curriculum development, but they were also responsible for advice on appointments, equipment, furnishing and building design. A wise head would 'court' the advisory team if he/she wanted additional staff, new furniture or building adaptation, in addition to curriculum advice! They rarely 'inspected' schools as such, but their visits were often seen as occasions when professionals would exchange views and by putting in a growth point or two, the adviser would leave, only to return a few weeks later to see whether or not the point made had been taken up.

Advisory teams became very powerful and until very recently, that power base had not been threatened. The numbers of advisers grew (for example, in Northamptonshire between 1974 and 1990 by four times) and with this growth a split occurred between the function of monitoring (or inspection) and the function of giving advice. Some LEAs made strenuous efforts to keep the two together but, with the development of in-service education, it was almost inevitable that the inspectors as they were often now called, would be supplemented by teams of advisory teachers, the best of whom had a profound influence on the classroom practice of an enormous number of teachers.

This expansion had been triggered by the 1972 White Paper, *A Framework for Expansion*, which recognized the need for a large and systematic expansion of in-service education, a planned induction process and the achievement of an all-graduate profession. It was envisaged that through these methods, the teaching profession would be well prepared both academically and profession-ally 'to guide each generation of children and enhance their intellectual capabilities'. The concept of school-focused training was established, allied to the work of teachers' centres and the expansion of the advisory teacher framework.

It is surprising to see how recently the power of local authorities reached its zenith, and how rapidly that power has been taken away. The statutory responsibility of a local authority for the content and quality of education in its schools was made clear in the Department of Education and Science (DES) publication *The School Curriculum* (March 1981), and was further emphasized in DES Circulars 6/81 and 8/83 within which each LEA was charged with reviewing its policy for the school curriculum and the extent to which current provision in schools was consistent with that policy. Progress was slow, and whilst some LEAs were responding very positively, this was not so in all. There were difficulties. Whilst LEAs had a responsibility to formulate curricular policies and objectives which met national policies and objectives and could be applied by each school to its own circumstances, it was left to individual schools to shape the curriculum for each pupil. As was stated in *The School Curriculum*, 'Neither the government nor local authorities should specify in detail what the schools should teach. This is for the schools themselves to determine.' LEAs, advised on the curriculum by their advisory service, formu-lated broad policies, but the detail and content were left to the individual school.

Parents were perplexed. Why was it that pupils in a school within the same authority were receiving a somewhat different curriculum and also, why were there differences between authorities? What made a good school? How import-ant were 'results'? Central government was also asking questions. Why was it that in international comparisons English students appeared to do less well than our European neighbours? Further, was there not an entitlement for all pupils and students to receive a common curriculum?

Thus the notion of a National Curriculum was born. Schools would follow a common prescribed curriculum which left the individual school to determine how that curriculum should be taught, the teaching methods and organization.

All children would be tested, using national tests at the end of each 'key' stage, that is at 7, 11, 14 and 16 years, although what made a 'key' stage each with its varying lengths of time, and each with its own curriculum, was never explained.

In terms of what makes a good school and, perhaps more importantly, what to do about a 'failing' school, the inspection of schools on a regular basis was seen to be of particular importance. Performance indicators, be they attendance rates, exclusion rates or examination results, were seen as crude indicators and inspection was seen as informing on the qualitative aspect of schools, their curricula, organization, classroom practice and management.

By removing, by and large, decisions about the curriculum content from schools, ways were sought of giving them more direct means of implementing that curricula. The introduction of local management of schools (LMS) was seen to be the way in which schools could retain some of their power. Circular 7/88 (paragraph 10) sets out clearly the underlying principle that schemes of local management should secure maximum delegation of financial responsibilities to governing bodies consistent with the discharge of their statutory responsibilities. The role of the LEA in terms of 'purse-holder' was being eroded, although the LEA was seen to have a responsibility for the professional development of its teachers (paragraph 19), pump priming for curricular development (paragraph 90), advice on appointments and dismissals (paragraph 134), for effective monitoring of a school's financial arrangements (paragraph 151) and for improving the quality of teaching and learning in its schools (paragraph 155). Inspection was to be carried out on a four-yearly basis by a new organization, the Office for Standards in Education (OFSTED), which would recruit and train a new inspectorate. LEAs could still carry out their own inspections, but from September 1994 and certainly by 1998, these will be hardly necessary if the national system is in place and working.

Such a system is costly and LEAs will have a proportion of their expenditure 'top-sliced' from the gross budget for education to cover the costs of inspection. Thus, schools will not be required to cover the direct costs of inspection, but there will be recommendations which governing bodies will be expected to follow up and, indeed, to provide an action plan and schools will have to finance these and related activities from their own budgets.

A further issue arises over inspection. The establishment of independent teams of inspectors operating at 'arm's length' from schools and across LEA boundaries suggests the need for an inspection service which is large enough to fulfil the conditions laid down by OFSTED. Are there sufficient numbers of highly qualified people from LEA advisory services who can fulfil these conditions? If not, where will the team members come from? Probably, the schools themselves will be asked to provide potential inspectors, but this would have profound implications for schools. How would parents react, for example, if the most senior and respected teachers were being taken away from duties in their schools to inspect schools elsewhere, and whilst such an arrangement might appear financially advantageous, staff replacement costs could be high.

Is inspection of any use if it is not followed by worthwhile advice? Worthwhile advice is difficult to give without first having closely observed what is happening in the classroom. Secretary of State Baker acknowledged this in 1988 when he stated that 'a balance must be kept between inspection and advice' and that support must be given to schools and teachers 'to help them find their way through the uncertainties and anxieties which change so often brings in its wake' (quoted in Scholey, 1990). Furthermore, the relationship between the school, its teachers and whoever is giving the advice is critical. Knowing the school well is an essential prerequisite of not only giving good advice, but also of that advice being acted upon. Without a climate of trust between the partners, little can be achieved. This advice will need to be paid for. With extended delegation of schools (for example, 98 per cent for all middle and secondary schools in Northamptonshire), the LEA will have little chance of providing such a service without the full co-operation of schools on a buy-back system.

The National Curriculum is not the whole curriculum. If one takes the Taylor definition from the 1977 DES publication *A New Partnership for Our Schools*, it can be noted that the school curriculum is seen as being wide and all-embracing: 'the school curriculum effectively comprehends the sum of experiences to which a child is exposed at school'. This suggests that there is a place for experiences other than those contained within the National Curriculum. Further, the National Curriculum is subject to change through review, and reshaping as a consequence. Thus there is still a place for curriculum development where universities and institutes of higher education provide the research frameworks which schools, aided by advisory services, are enabled to develop. The curriculum is not static, but is constantly evolving in an attempt to meet the future needs of society in general. Recent developments illustrate this trend, particularly those relating to the moral and spiritual dimension of society, and to the work-related curriculum with involvement by such bodies as the Training and Enterprise Council (TEC).

Outside views, given the relationship mentioned earlier, can be helpful to a school whenever evaluation is required. The school development plan is a very powerful tool which forms an integral part of a school's accountability procedures and should help the school establish priorities. It will be important for a school to look beyond its boundaries and to be sure that the development plan is of quality. An advisory service can be a useful enabler when clustering arrangements are in hand and when issues of continuity are being addressed. It should also be able to give schools indications on qualitative aspects of their plans.

The school development plans should also be useful instruments in providing LEAs with information in determining priorities within its strategic planning role and resource provision. An advisory services function will be to monitor and evaluate the work of schools, and report to committee on issues which arise. This will be an important aspect of the work of the advisory services as committee composition is subject to change with local elections, and it will be to the advisory services through the chief officers that members will turn for advice and guidance.

In order to provide a service to schools and the wider community, local authority advisory services, if they are to survive, will need to be sharper and more cost-effective. Direct contact with schools is essential if advice given is to be meaningful, and accurate, up-to-date information and sound evaluation will be required if chief officers and members are to be kept well informed. If schools and the LEA feel that this partnership is worth having, the advisory services will continue to play an important part in the education service. The dilemma, however, is how this can be achieved with inspection of schools as part of the total function of a service. If inspection is part of the team brief, how will this affect the ability to give advice and support to schools, and will advice and support debar inspectors/advisory teachers from inspecting? How 'close' the 'close relationship' is between inspectors and schools will have to be tested in the courts, but it appears that a link inspector will be deemed to have had a close relationship with a school. The test will come when a school (or perhaps a neighbouring school) objects to a certain inspection team member on the grounds of 'close relationship'.

It is suggested that there will be a continuing need for an LEA advisory service which could well have an inspection branch as part of this, in addition to a branch for management, curriculum advice and support, and a branch relating to monitoring and evaluation. The crucial question is whether or not LEAs and schools would be prepared to support such a structure as costs could be high.

Costs to the LEA for service-level agreements can be met if the following conditions are present:

- the advisory service is seen as an organization whose overheads have been reduced – such organizations have, in the past, had high overheads due to the nature of their work and the support systems which have been established;
- the LEA does not delegate such a high percentage of its budget that there is little left for the operation of such a service within an LEA;
- the number of grant-maintained schools within an authority is a low percentage of the total schools.

Costs to schools also might appear high and if schools are to 'buy in', they will want to be assured of value for money. Governing bodies might find budgeting for advice and guidance services difficult. Governing bodies will apply their funding allocation in the most efficient and effective way to maximize benefits to pupils, but first call on budgets will continue to be for staffing purposes. The call for a greater proportion of non-contact time for primary teachers will place a further strain on budgets, and some schools might well be tempted to cut expenditure on in-service activities which, if followed through by a large number of schools, would place the whole operation in jeopardy.

While the Grants for Education Support and Training (GEST) scheme is in operation, some safeguard is available as these funds are provided specifically for curriculum development and, although the definition of 'development' is wide, GEST funding is a source of income for advisory services.

What are the kinds of service-level agreement which might operate between an advisory service, the LEA and its schools? One way in which they might be thought of is by devising agreements within three categories:

- for schools, where the LEA pays;
- for the LEA, where the LEA pays; and
- for schools, where schools pay.

In the first category will be curriculum services and training which the LEA feels are important enough to fund with the aid of developed GEST funds to schools. These will include 'basic curriculum' courses and activities, and the upkeep of resource bases for most areas of the curriculum. Also in this category will be certain initiatives such as training and support for schools which implement Records of Achievement.

A second area for schools in which the LEA pays will be in management services and training and will cover areas such as:

- advice to governors and selection panels for headteacher and deputy headteacher appointments;
- observation and investigations relating to teacher competencies;
- the provision of management training and a consultancy service for schools;
- mentoring of newly appointed headteachers, supplementing the mentoring scheme funded by GEST;
- support for newly qualified and licensed teachers by peripatetic professional tutors in the primary phase and by subject specialist advisers for secondary teachers;
- help for supply teachers and teachers returning to the classroom in updating classroom skills and knowledge of recent developments in teaching;
- personal professional advice to teachers;
- assistance to LEA headteacher groups, where the advisory service through its senior advisers facilitates, negotiates agendas, assists in the organization and provides expert consultation as agreed with individual groups;
- management of centrally organized activities such as swimming, sports, foreign language assistants, arts and theatre curricular provision;
- the upkeep of Professional Development Centres.

Services for the LEA where the LEA pays could include:

- curricular advice to enable members and officers to carry out their functions which could include statutory duties related to National Curriculum Assessment, statistical collation and analysis of results and preparation of reports for committee;
- sample surveys of schools to inform on specific aspects;
- advice to the LEA on a range of policies and issues such as the European Dimension, Children Act, special educational needs;
- a link inspector network with an agenda from the LEA in order to monitor specific activities;
- provision of representatives for inter-agency work;
- appropriate expertise for the LEA to make provision for children with special educational needs;
- managing the provision for ethnic minority pupils and other section 11(6) responsibilities relating to teaching and non-teaching staff support for pupils of New Commonwealth heritage;
- managing the GEST programme and securing its successful implementation;
- contributing to the appraisal scheme for headteachers;
- building design, including specification of educational requirements for school accommodation improvements.

Service-level agreements for schools where schools pay will result from very delicate negotiations. Once again, a sound relationship between the advisory service and the school is paramount. Where this has been built up over a number of years by a known and respected member of the advisory team, then there is every chance of success. It is where such a relationship has not been achieved that problems could arise.

Schools will also need to be confident that the advisory service has obtained some nationally recognized award for the quality of service. Here, teams would be well advised to consider such schemes as 'Investors in People' (IIP) or obtaining a British Standard (BS) 5750 Kite Mark.

A scheme which might be devised could have two tiers, a full service agreement and a subscription-level service. In the full service agreement, there could be full access to all advisory service facilities, training courses, consultancy and management services at no additional charge. Additional benefits might be given to those with a full service agreement, for example, priority when booking courses or personnel for consultancy. A subscription-level service, on the other hand, would provide information and advice at a more general level, along with updates, information and advice at regular intervals.

Charges for these two schemes would need to take account of a school's ability to pay and as the LMS formula is pupil-led, then it follows that size of school must be taken into account. In addition, the phase within which the school operates should be taken into consideration due to the different weightings of pupil units. A further consideration might be to base the subscription on the number of staff, on the assumption that more staff could well mean greater use of advisory service personnel and activities. These are all issues which advisory teams will have to come to terms with if they are to continue to provide a quality service to schools.

In order to deliver such a service to schools, to the LEA and to OFSTED, a well-qualified and dedicated team of professionals will be required. If the scale of service is ambitious the team will, of necessity, be large. Each curriculum area will require expertise within a phase, and initiatives such as special educational needs will require cross-curricular teams. It is, therefore, difficult to see a fully integrated service operating successfully with less than a team of 100 advisers and 40 support staff, and this must have implications for small LEAs which would find it difficult to have a service-level agreement to sustain that size of team. Furthermore, the fewer the number of schools in an authority, the higher the costs of an advisory service per school. This also applies to authorities where schools do not take out full service-level agreements. Obviously, the size of the authority is crucial within the framework.

An advisory and inspection service, to be successful, will aim to provide a high-quality service to schools. This will include consultancy, training, management consultancy and inspection services for schools and for the LEA. The organization will have a vision in which a high standard of education is sustained and developed whatever the individual learning needs might be.

This can best be achieved through co-operation and collaboration (rather than by competition) within a community of committed professionals engaged in curriculum, management and development. Successful organizations depend on a high level of staff development and external consultancy. The policy of the service must be to employ expert staff and make further training possible for them, to adjust to the needs of schools as a result of systematic communication and by quick response to requests.

Given the conditions outlined above, there is every reason to believe that school improvement will continue. There is a place for LEAs and their advisory services in the future, although the myth of the 'cosy relationship between LEAs, their schools, advisers and inspectors', mentioned by the Prime Minister in the House of Commons on 3 July 1991, will have to be nailed. Some circles see this relationship as not being in the interests of raising the quality of education through higher expectations. However, without this relationship it is going to be difficult, if not impossible, to attain the standards sought. To destroy an organization and structure which has developed over nearly a century would leave many schools feeling isolated. There *is* value in being a member of a family, and it does not follow that the relationships are cosy!

LEA schools and self-managing realities

For Part II, headteachers were invited to write about topics in the running of individual schools which had assumed particular self-managing significance for them during the period following the introduction of local management of schools in 1992. Within the limitations of one book it was clear from the outset that not every issue could be tackled by the contributors but it was believed their experience during the early period of unprecedented change would reflect concerns and priorities found in many secondary schools.

Thus, this part includes contributions from headteachers who found that the new context for the governance and management of educational endeavour in schools not only focused on issues of efficiency in financial resource management to promote the teaching and learning objectives of schools but also on the achievement of improved effectiveness, and understanding of the processes involved, in the deployment of financial and human resources.

CHAPTER 4

Local management of schools: professional partnership and financial gains

JOHN HOWELLS

In a chapter on local management of schools within an enduring LEA partnership, John Howells provides an overview of the processes involved in developing an LMS framework not only to secure organizational efficiency but also to promote positive attitudes towards genuine partnership and accountability relationships with the governing body of the school. He demonstrates the emergence of a clear sense of 'ownership' in the sharing of responsibilities for effective management through the delegation of authority among teaching and administrative staff, to achieve greater collective effectiveness in the realities of priority planning for the phased development of a self-managing school on a continuous basis.

The context of change

The past twenty years have seen a change in the role of the headteacher from the leading educationalist *primus inter pares* to a different sort of professional, much more concerned with issues of management of the institution. This process has been considerably speeded up by the introduction of local management of schools (LMS).

The change towards a greater degree of site management is not confined to the UK or to the world of education. It is one of a series of changes which run as themes through this period, including increased parent power, relevance to economic needs and preoccupation with testing. In the UK there has also been a conflict between the relative powers of central government, local authority and the school's governing body. This conflict has been highlighted by the introduction of LMS, so that any discussion of the cost of the introduction of such a scheme, balanced against its benefits, has often seemed less important than the political agenda of who has power in the management of schools and the control of the curriculum. Is this a decision for educators, for politicians alone or for a partnership of the two? At the time of writing politicians seem reluctant to share decisions, or even to consult, with the professionals. As a result proposals have often been unworkable in a real school situation. Even the School Curriculum and Assessment Authority (SCAA) has educational representation only as appointed by the Secretary of State.

Headteachers have not willingly relinquished their power to influence the curriculum directly. The offer, in exchange, to influence the allocation of resources within the school has often seemed a marginal benefit and has required time-consuming and occasionally uncomfortable re-skilling. A greater responsibility for control of the budget has also brought the need to share those management decisions with governors, whose interest may be in only part of schools' tasks. Some governors have brought considerable financial expertise, although not always directly transferable. Others have needed even more re-skilling than the headteacher, without the time available to devote to it. The uncomfortable situation of control by committed amateurs over professional management decisions has been brought into much higher focus by the needs of LMS. It is debatable how much power has in reality been passed to heads in exchange for their loss of influence over the curriculum.

In theory the budget has given control of other resources – the hours and rates of pay of non-teaching staff, redefinition of roles, etc. – but in practice the unavoidable demands of fixed costs for premises and existing staff have left very little surplus for creative flexibility in the area of capitation. In the first year of LMS, after a long and detailed study of the issues involved, one chair of governors offered a graphic description of the reality of our new-found power as 'half a baked bean'. Four budgets later we clearly have much more flexibility but the workload and the hidden 'opportunity cost' has been prodigious, both for senior staff and for overworked and underpaid non-teaching staff.

The LEA took on extra staff, computerized the accounting system, offered optimistic 'awareness-raising' INSET, successively refined the list of discretionary exceptions and, under pressure, introduced cheque book facilities for all except staffing costs. Most recently Oxfordshire LEA increased devolution of funds beyond the 1995 target of 90 per cent of the general schools' budget. Oxfordshire's commitment to consultation cannot be faulted! Hard-pressed heads and bemused governors filled in a 70-page questionnaire on the proposed changes – their implications for schools and their budgets. A formidable task of analysis for the LEA! The result was less radical than expected, with the majority of schools in effect buying back most of the LEA services offered:

> Quality Schools Association (advisers)
> Education management and administration
> Resource Plus (including library service)
> Payroll administration

Maternity leave insurance
Other insurances
Remedial tree work
County purchasing
In-county residential centre
Property services
IT training and support
Administration Plus
The position of peripatetic music and out-county residential centres
was to be put to consultation in 1994.

There have been times in the past few years when the pace and frequency of change in response to central government policies brought very forcibly to mind the comments attributed to the Roman author Gaius Petronius:

> We trained hard but it seemed that every time we were beginning to form up teams, we would be reorganised. I was to learn later in life that we tend to meet any new situation by reorganising and a wonderful method it can be for creating the illusion of progress whilst producing confusion, inefficiency and demoralisation.

Patterns of change

The pattern of change of which LMS is both a symptom and a contributory cause has been concerned with priorities in education policies and has influenced the roles of the key participants. Priorities have changed. Because of the pre-eminence of the age-weighted pupil unit (AWPU) ratio, schools' entry policies have become more significant and there is a risk that the need for publicity will make increasing demands on limited funds on the grounds that 'you have to speculate in order to accumulate'; competition for clients between neighbouring schools is clearly encouraged. These were not major issues for headteachers a generation ago, but we ignore them today at our peril. Special needs has also gained a higher profile, with a close watch kept on the money spent on special needs compared with the income generated by the various formulae: not an approach which sits easily on any teacher, headteachers included.

Community education also finds itself in a difficult position of having to justify itself and pay its way, at the risk of being marginalized if it is not cost-effective. The fear of spending, or mis-spending, the limited funds allocated for pupils' education has forced caution upon headteachers who would previously have done all in their power to encourage the use of school resources by the community and to spread the concept of lifelong learning among pupils. New ideas for development in the community now have to be greeted, if not out loud, with the thought of 'what is it going to cost the school if we let this happen'.

The whole issue of the delegation of funds through local management to schools themselves has been clouded by a series of cuts in educational spending over the last five years. It has often seemed that the whole concept of devolving responsibility was a political device to put on to other shoulders the responsibility for making unpopular decisions about cuts and economies. As G. Handscomb (1991) remarks: 'The expectation that LMS would liberate schools to manage monies more efficiently was certainly strong, particularly among senior managers, but was tempered by disappointment about the reality of underfunding' (p.110).

The reordering of priorities has required some clearer thinking about policies. Unfortunately much of that thinking has been required to be done from first principles by each school and a great deal of headteacher time over the last few years has been devoted to writing policies which had previously been implicit. A typical example is the school's policy on charging for school visits in order to ensure that the school complies with the 1988 Act, without the resources to be as generous as it would like to support parents at a time of economic constraint. School use of residential centres has had to be critically re-examined, the county Music Service is worryingly at risk, we have had to think very carefully about our use of foreign language assistants, about the funding of cross-phase links and policies for link courses with colleges, previously paid separately. Pupils have usually lost out in this 'reallocation' of resources.

We have to count too the cost of involvement with initial teacher training and risk ruining good relationships with colleges by asking how much they will pay us to take their students. Money is set aside each year for in-service training but one important element has become a casualty. A school will try to fund INSET which is seen to be directly relevant to its own needs as an institution but staff seeking professional development on a wider front will increasingly find themselves funding it themselves. The old pattern of secondments which might lead to a change in career direction are unlikely to be seen by a school as an investment; why pay money to lose a promising member of staff?

However uncomfortable the time-scale, the reordering of priorities and the counting of opportunity costs have brought obvious gains to the effective and efficient management of schools. LMS has brought more direct management gains too: flexibility to act early on staff appointments and to respond locally and quickly to repairs to premises, an increase in clerical staff time to help cope with LMS administration, a firm commitment to learning support assistants' time for a whole year (instead of termly confirmation) and, most obviously, an increase in departmental capitation in response to the needs of the National Curriculum. All these were achieved in spite of LEA budget cuts each year. The main savings have been on grounds maintenance and equipment contracts, which were very generously paid for when centralized. The supply teacher budget also allows savings in a normal year.

The most challenging part of the pattern of change brought about by LMS is the effect on the roles of people involved with schools. Implicit in all the comments so far is the changed role of the headteacher, usually imposed upon heads already in office and affecting fundamentally tasks, relationships and career decisions. Deputy heads and senior teachers have had to take on a greater concern with management, as distinct from, and probably in addition to, administration. This is a move which many of them have welcomed.

The potential change in the role of heads of department is almost as radical. The principle of devolution of responsibility from the LEA to schools can be extended and the same model used within a school. Individual departments become autonomous cost centres. Capitation devolved to them includes responsibility not only for the normal range of capitation expenses, books, consumables, etc. but for departmental travel and INSET, maintenance for department rooms, paying for supply cover and, potentially the most valuable of all, for increasing hours and expertise of non-teaching staff. If the languages department has a budget which must include the cost of language assistants, will it still be quite so insistent when the alternative might be a part-time qualified teacher for the whole of the year? If the geography department budget includes an allocation for residential field study centres, will it still use the county provision or seek cheaper alternatives? If departments have to pay for their own cover from this increased allocation, will that encourage or curtail attendance on in-service training courses during the school day? This principle could be extended to include cost centres other than traditional subject departments. Listed below are 1993 budget headings other than staff and premises, administered by the bursar, but each monitored by a senior member of staff (nine colleagues are responsible for at least one account other than a subject department or faculty):

Supplies and services accounts

Staff-related expenses
Interviews/advertising
Staff travel
INSET
Local travel
Government training
GEST: teacher appraisal
Interns (ITT)

Faculties
Arts
Communications
Humanities
Maths/Technology
Science
Cross-curricular: PSE, careers, etc.
Curriculum development
Assessment/records

Library and resources: IT
FE link courses

Support
Educational equipment purchased
Educational equipment maintained
Exam fees
Classroom furniture
Minibus
Community links
Bursary funding (subsidies to students)

Administration
Computer system costs
Telephone/post
Administration consumables
Printing/brochures/newsletter
Contingency fund

The effect of LMS upon advisers and LEA officers has been very considerable and is dealt with in other chapters. One outcome has been the removal of the special funds which advisers administered, sometimes perhaps rather partially! A small advantage to set against the acceleration of the move from their role as local authority advisers to inspectors. This was a predictable, almost inevitable, effect of the changes in local responsibilities and accountability.

The governors' role too has undergone a radical change. The old-style governor, probably a former pupil, with local knowledge of the school and its parents who offered support and encouragement to heads in their professional tasks now seems much more than just a generation distant. Governors are expected to bring some outside expertise. They are expected to be willing to be trained. They are expected to give up a great deal of time to understand the complexities of managing a school, attending sub-committee meetings, studying account sheets, reading background documents, responding to rapidly changing government initiatives and weighing up the financial implications of the headteacher's recommendations. Many people active in the community who would make excellent, supportive governors have no stomach for this new role and the education service is the poorer for it.

Mechanisms for change

There have been four significant mechanisms through which schools have changed their style of management in recent years, partly as a direct result of the introduction of LMS but also in response to the wider influences which made LMS seem like an appropriate development in the late 1980s. These four mechanisms for change are the creation of smaller specialist committees to structure the increased involvement of governors; the extension of the role of the school management team; the need to create a clear and evolving development plan; and the separation of administration functions from management by increased use of support staff.

Governors

School governors are either elected (by parents/staff), nominated by local political parties, or co-opted. Traditionally they saw themselves as a support to the 'managers' of the school; they are also now expected to be a check upon them, the body to which the head is primarily accountable. But they, along with the head, are also accountable to the elected representatives of the LEA and, increasingly, directly to the DFE. It would be surprising if this ambivalence did not affect the relationship between head and governors. The perception of the board of governors as the body to whom the head is increasingly accountable has been encouraged by government. The day-to-day management of the school clearly remains with the head and staff, but in the name of local democracy governors have been assigned a role which is sometimes beyond their expertise. Headteachers often feel that giving governors adequate 'context' and keeping them informed is as much an energy trap as a help. We and they worry about what they will be expected to have to make decisions about next. It seems right and proper that governors should be concerned in long-term budget-setting, school policies, grievance procedures and local community involvement. In theory they can intervene in any aspect of running the school. As a DES instruction booklet entitled *School Governors: A Guide to the Law* (1992) puts it:

> A good head will discuss all the main aspects of school life with the governors and expect them to offer general guidance. . . . Governors have a right to ask the head for a report on anything that goes on at the school, provided the head is given a reasonable amount of time to put this together.

The full governing body of more than twenty people meeting once a term is a difficult group for detailed study of issues and decision-making and the elected staff are not necessarily those with relevant expert knowledge to contribute to the decision-making process. Most schools have therefore set up committees of governors and staff. A typical list of governor sub-committees and their areas of concern is attached (see Appendix 4.1 at the end of this chapter). This framework gives good opportunities for representation of teaching and non-teaching staff. Such meetings are often working meetings with a shared task rather than presentation of cut-and-dried options for governors to accept or challenge. Governors can therefore specialize and become expert in one area of the school's activity, and the danger of an inner circle of powerful governors is reduced by wider involvement. The disadvantages are that the servicing of these sub-committees becomes a major task for the senior members of staff who act as conveners. Agendas, minutes, background documents, etc. all take a great deal of time and it is not always possible to arrange for non-teaching staff to do the secretarial work. It is, however, a very effective mechanism for in-service training of governors.

School management team

Once upon a time, headteachers met once a week with the deputy heads to check on who was taking responsibility for what and that nothing was being done twice. As pressure increased, many heads felt it necessary to meet once a day. If the load of management decisions, servicing governors, etc. is not to become an intolerable burden on the head and deputies, other senior staff must become increasingly involved. Certainly the differential in pay between deputy heads and senior teachers is no longer sufficient to suggest an unbridgeable gap in expectations. The school's 'senior management team' may have eight or more members, each with whole-school responsibilities for some aspect of management – curriculum, in-service training, monitoring pupil progress, publicity, links with community education; the team may also include a non-teaching/administrative member. The management team's role must be management. The purpose of the meetings is to make informed decisions. Meetings must be regular, frequent, properly minuted with advance agenda, discussion papers prepared, and routine or purely administrative tasks delegated to individuals and not endlessly 'evaluated' or revised. A large management team can also function very well through a series of smaller teams – deputy head and senior teacher responsible for curriculum – pastoral deputy working with senior teacher responsible for careers or special needs. The agenda of senior management team meetings should reflect management concerns, the implications of which will subsequently be disseminated through separate pastoral and curriculum boards – heads of year and heads of faculty. Below is a list of the roles of members of the senior management team and a typical agenda for one of its fortnightly meetings:

Senior Management Team
Headteacher
Deputy Head: Curriculum and resources
Deputy Head: Assessment and pastoral care
Records and evaluation (Head of Communications Faculty)
Professional Tutor/INSET (Head of Science Faculty)
Timetable (Head of Mathematics/Technology Faculty)
PSE Co-ordinator – Head of Learning Support
Head of Faculty: Creative Arts
Chief Administration Officer (Minutes)
Head of Community Education in attendance

Senior Management Team – 20 January 1992

Standing Agenda:

(a)   Curriculum matters and Resources
(b)   Assessment and monitoring
(c)   Finance
(d)   Evaluation
(e)   Links with governors

Open Agenda:

1.   Advisers' consultancy visit – 9–11 March
2.   Principles governing allocation of tutors for 1993/94
3.   Forecast grades – Year 11 (re Deputy Head's note)
4.   Youth Award scheme
5.   Alternative Curriculum Week (12–16 July 1993): Years 8 and 9
6.   Cross-phase issues
7.   Key Stage 4 Technology and options
8.   Devolved funding.

The school development plan

The purpose of a school development plan is twofold. It can be both a means
of public accountability and a management tool for future developments. The
school staff are likely to see the latter as by far the more important objective
although a clearly presented and updated plan can also inform people outside
the school who support its work and carry some responsibility for its oversight.
A development plan must clearly be an ongoing process as targets are achieved
or agenda and resources vary but there have to be milestones along the road
of development, a clear statement of long-term plans which is the basis of
subsequent modification.

There is a move towards schools having business plans. A development plan
should be more than this, with a strong element of institutional self-evaluation.
The received wisdom disseminated at management courses suggests that for
change to be successful, there has to be a degree of 'ownership', a recognition
by the people involved that the change is necessary to improve performance.
Development plans are in this tradition and therefore, in the present climate,
possibly doomed to obsolescence.

In terms of accountability schools have been involved in a series of other
monitoring processes including HMI inspections, publication of examination
results, INSET plans and TVEI accreditation. In recent years, the submission
of budget proposals to the LEA, annual reports of governors to parents and
the regulations governing school prospectuses, as well as the regular OFSTED
inspections, have all added to the way in which schools are expected to be
accountable to their parents and the elected representatives of the LEA. The
introduction of LMS has clearly contributed to this process, both through the
involvement of governors and the annual publication of reports on progress
and expenditure.

LMS has also contributed to the use of a school development plan as a means of improving school performance. Development requires resources. The development plan becomes the blueprint for priorities. The difficulty lies in achieving the appropriate balance between process and product in forward planning. The product is clearly the plan on paper, the written list of 'smart' objectives, the charts and matrices of what is to be achieved by when, by whom and how, and such a plan should include a consideration of how it is all going to be paid for. It can only be done if each constituent part has given due consideration to the needs of the whole and the process has directly involved the people who must make it work. A development plan produced by the headteacher over half-term will be of very limited value! Budget-holders must produce their part of the plan themselves to a common template. Appropriate outside agencies, governors, partner primary schools, parents and local employers should be involved if possible. Improvements envisaged must be those which the departments concerned recognize as worthwhile and necessary, the cost weighed against the advantage and against other opportunities which could have been bought with those resources.

The one-page extract from a school's development plan, given in Appendix 4.2 at the end of the chapter, shows targets for development. This is additional to a 16-point summary of proposals for the next four years for development of the curriculum (National Curriculum, post-16 courses, cross-curricular themes, etc.).

The construction of a development plan can be seen as a microcosm of local management, with the additional cost implicit in managing one's own resources weighed against the perceived benefit for the department or the whole school.

Administrative officer/bursar

The devolution of funds to schools through LMS was not accompanied by adequate money for administration of those funds. For the first two or three years, central staff at County Hall had more rather than less work in analysing former patterns of expenditure, training school accounts secretaries, preparing appropriate software, offering advice, 'raising awareness' of governors, etc. Staff were already in post at County Hall so that was where they remained. Schools had to fend for themselves in staffing terms and were told that since money was devolved by LMS they could now make their own decisions about how it could be spent. In practice it meant taking money away from direct educational uses to increase hours and salaries of non-teaching staff, for which heads had long been campaigning. The difficult decision was passed on to headteachers – to pay the bursar more for more work at the expense of textbooks.

Governors felt that there was an undue proportion of administrative work being done by highly paid experts – heads and deputy heads. They also felt that there was the potential for expanding business opportunities in a school, most obviously through use of premises, and that this was an inappropriate addition to existing workloads. If a person could be appointed for administration and entrepreneurial initiative, in theory they might more than pay for themselves in a year by increasing income. Some schools, in an act of faith, appointed an administrative officer to oversee the non-teaching staff, monitor financial procedures and to seek to increase income. Typically such an appointment would be from outside the world of education and would certainly cost less than a deputy head: APT and C senior officer scale is equivalent to an MPG teacher at the top of the scale. The outside expertise is potentially a great advantage although in practice a good deal of in-service training is required to provide the necessary context for decisions which will affect, however indirectly, the education of the pupils.

It is possible that governors might expect someone with no background of classroom experience to feel more directly responsible to them than to the head. The situation is not unknown in independent schools, when economic constraints bring the bursar, directly accountable to the governors, into conflict with the headteacher's educational priorities.

Summarized below is the role of an administrative officer appointed in response to the pressure of work generated by LMS:

> **Responsibilities:** The Administrative Officer will be responsible to the Headteacher, have overall managerial control of the non-teaching aspects of the school and its administration, will meet regularly with the Head and will be a member of the Senior Management Team. He/ she will attend and report to governors' meetings.

Job description:
Finance and Accounting
Forward planning: Assist Head to prepare annual budget; explore and implement income-raising schemes; analyse costs to reduce expenditure; provide information for governors.
Day to day: Supervise finance personnel and financial routine; act as 'systems manager'; supervise premises-related budget allocation; advise/liaise with teaching staff over department finance.
Non-teaching Staff
Responsibility for welfare and career development; recruitment; records; compliance with employer legislation.
Buildings and Grounds
Day-to-day maintenance; long-term maintenance and redecorating schedules; monitor energy efficiency; liaison for letting of premises to outside bodies; liaise with sub-contractors on site, regular (cleaners and caterers) and occasional (builders, decorators, maintenance engineers).
General Administration
School office; reprographics, advice on current personnel legislation; liaise with teaching staff on use of buildings, school transport, publicity,

educational events, etc.; Health and Safety legislation; assist partner primary schools.

Conclusion

The aim of LMS was to give schools greater autonomy. It coincided in time with cuts in public expenditure which meant an increase in responsibility but no corresponding increase in resources. This led to some conflict with the LEA over cuts, AWPU ratios, special needs and the whole argument of how much was to be devolved and what retained at the centre. What has emerged is a different pattern of resource management in schools, with a move towards even greater devolution and more autonomous departments.

The claim that LMS gives greater autonomy for schools sits uneasily with the parallel changes in control of the curriculum, with schools being drawn into conflict directly with the DFE, over GCSE – the 'decline in standards', the withdrawal of coursework assessment, the lack of congruence with Key Stage 4 of the National Curriculum, and the lack of agreement in content – and even more in methodology, between courses and tests at Key Stage 3. Alongside the rhetoric of school autonomy and parent power, the changes in content and assessment of the National Curriculum, particularly in English and Technology, seem oddly inconsistent.

There is currently pressure for the financial autonomy of schools to be taken further, with the suggestion of logical progression from LMS to GM status, with schools being encouraged to opt out in order to gain financially. The gain looks to be only temporary and it is important to count the cost in terms of lost professional partnerships. The present arrangement for opting out will be gained only at the expense of other schools within the local authority. A school may be attracted by its full per capita allocation of special needs resources because that represents more than its current share. The reason may well be that other schools within the authority have a greater need because they have a different catchment area. Governors and headteachers should look at the profit and loss account not just in financial terms and offer appropriate leadership and guidance to parents. A local authority offers professional partnership with advisers and officers and some assurance of fairness in an admissions policy and the distribution of resources across a whole area, not just for the limited catchment of one school.

The latest phase of LMS, with more than 90 per cent of the general schools' budget share delegated, brings a greater need for partnership with other headteachers in neighbouring secondary schools, and increasingly important pressure for partnerships between secondary and primary schools. A future pattern may move towards sharing costs of previous LEA provision – a shared bursar, perhaps, common policies for special needs or community education.

The thrust of LMS is that schools should be more businesslike, more competitive, concentrating on image and public relations, satisfied customers and measured products, marketable in the nation's economy, risking bankruptcy, avoiding co-operation and insisting on only the best quality raw materials. Such business objectives bear little relation to the agreed aims of most schools. What do we want to control resources for? Greater management efficiency must lead to more effective pupil learning. The simplistic view of schools as businesses competing in the market place is within easy leaping distance of the idea that 'if it can't be measured, it isn't worth doing. . .'.

The measure of our success must be of a very long-term product: success seen in the quality of the process – the 'incremental' gain – hard to measure or to boast about, but recognizable in the growing skills and knowledge of pupils as well as in their self-esteem and enthusiasm for study, to the benefit of themselves as well as the nation's economy.

Appendix 4.1: Governors' Sub-Committees

Terms of Reference: To work with staff in support of the school's development in the areas indicated.
To make appropriate reports and recommendations to the full Governing Body.
Meetings usually once per term.
One representative to be a member of the Policy & Finance Committee.

1. Curriculum
Governors: Four Governors
Staff support: Deputy Head and three staff.

          1. What is taught – breadth and balance.
          2. Sixth Form provision.
          3. Methodology – range of teaching/learning strategies.
          4. Resources for learning.
          5. Assessment – monitoring progress, external exams.
          6. Differentiation – special needs – most able.
          7. Cross-curricular – including Equal Opportunities; gender, class, race.

2. External Affairs
Governors: Four Governors
Staff support: Deputy Head and three staff.

          1. CEC (Community Education Council) and the wider community.
          2. Cross-phase work – partnership, other schools, colleges (incl. FE).
          3. External agencies and LEA services.
          4. Industry links and sponsorship.
          5. Careers – guidance; conventions; work experience.
          6. Public relations and press.
          7. Local councillors, MPs, etc.
          8. Governor Training.
          9. Liaison with the PTA.

3. Staffing

Governors: Five Governors

Staff support: Head, CAO, Professional Tutor, Non-teaching representative. (See
                        Annex A of Pay Policy document for detailed terms of reference.)

1. Teaching staff – structure and appointments.
2. Non-teaching staff.
3. Review of Pay Policy.
4. Job descriptions and conditions of service.
5. Staff development policy/INSET.
(There is a separate Grievance Committee.)

4. Premises

Governors: Four Governors

Staff support: CAO and three staff.

1. Health and Safety.
2. Letters and income.
3. Buildings maintenance, extensions.
4. Services – energy, water, refuse.
5. Caretakers, cleaners, catering.
6. Grounds (competitive tenders/contracts).

Policy & Finance Committee

Governors: Chairman and Vice-Chairman plus one representative from each Sub-
                        Committee.

Staff support: Headteacher, Deputy Heads, CAO.

The purpose of the Policy & Finance Committee is to set and oversee the broad direction
of policies and finance for the school and act as a communications channel between the
full Governing Body and the constituent Sub-Committees.

Appendix 4.2: Summary of Targets for Development

Monitoring Pupil Progress

1. Establish and resource the new assessment procedures, Records of Achievement and individual action plans.
2. Monitor new support arrangements for less able as the LSD changes role, and offer appropriate challenge to the most able.
3. Maintain a range of extra-curricular activities, with minimum disruption to classes or need for 'cover'.
4. Improve examination results.
   (a) At 16+ aim at 50% overall ABC pass rate, improving humanities results in particular, and aiming for more girls in Design/Technology.
   (b) At 18+, improve take up in sciences, aim at a higher proportion of grade A passes and investigate alternatives to A level (especially languages).
5. Develop the work experience scheme – with a better scheme of employer evaluation and extension to sixth form.

Resources for Learning

Management

1. Look for ways of increasing income under LMS – Trust Fund – sponsorship – lettings – more students.
2. Appoint a Bursar to handle administrative tasks and review the role and composition of the Senior Management Team.

Staffing

3. Set up a structure and initial training/awareness for Staff Appraisal.
4. Provide INSET for post-16 developments – guidance, core skills – action plans – and for delivery of the National Curriculum to the whole ability range.

Premises/Equipment

5. Pursue scheme for joint use of sports facilities with West Oxfordshire District Council.
6. Minor works to enlarge rooms for English and Maths.
7. Compete and equip the Media Studio.
8. Up-grade and extend the Nimbus computer network.
9. Modernize the reprographic facilities.
10. Provide more books for the library and increase its use – and set up a scheme for self-supported study.

Community

- Work with CEC on range of joint school/community courses.
- Increase the number of departments organizing Industry Days.
- Advertise the school more effectively by spending money on better brochures.
- Build on good primary school relations by sharing a liaison teacher for cross-phase curricular links.
- Encourage more governor involvement through working parties – trust fund – sponsorship – support group for PSE, village links and public relations.

CHAPTER 5

LMS – the orderly delegation of funds: the scramble for resources

MICHAEL FOSSEY

Within the general schools framework created for LMS, and exemplified by John Howells, Michael Fossey examines the ways in which the formulae for delegated budgets were developed in his LEA. In addition to devising models for establishing equitable criteria for funding entitlements between primary and secondary schools, consideration of developing a satisfactory model for the funding of special educational needs provision for pupils in neighbourhood schools has created major problems in many LEAs. This chapter outlines ways in which one LEA has attempted to make adequate and acceptable provision in an important area, but one that received little consideration or precision within the 'simple' national formulae of age-weighted pupil units (AWPUs).

Introduction

The requirement of the 1988 Education Act that a large proportion of schools should have delegated budgets with funds allocated by formula produced a flurry of activity in county halls, the purpose of which was to devise funding formulae which:

- met the requirement of the Act – that is, were objective and based on need rather than past history;
- met local needs – that is, produced budgets which reflected historical funding in order to prevent some schools being large-scale winners at the expense of others, who had become large-scale losers.

The gap between these irreconcilable aims was, in many cases, bridged by a transitional funding arrangement allowed by the Act. Subsequent legislation has extended delegation to most schools, and by April 1994 LEAs must delegate 90 per cent of the aggregated schools' budget with 80 per cent of that being calculated on the basis of pupil numbers, weighted for age and, where appropriate, special educational needs.

In a letter to all LEAs dated 2 June 1992, the Department of Education and Science (DES) (as it was) invited local authorities to consider simplification of existing formulae. The Secretary of State was said to be 'particularly concerned that some schemes contained complex formulae to deliver resources to take account of the incidence of Special Educational Needs or social deprivation. He will look to LEAs to justify the complexity or simplify the formulae.'

These two pressures, coupled with the need for higher levels of delegation and the prospect of a common funding formula for GM schools at least, will intensify the debate about the elements in any scheme for the distribution of resources.

Elements in the formulae and age-weighting

The AWPU, which is the major funding element in any scheme of delegation, is typically made up of a large number of items which are peculiar both in type and age-weighting to each authority, but in all schemes the single most important item is that for teaching costs. The crucial importance of the teaching cost element has caused it to be the focus of much dispute. The disputes have concentrated on the changes at phase boundaries with infant, junior, secondary and tertiary phases all crying 'Foul!' Perhaps the most bitter dispute has been over the primary/secondary boundary. A characteristic of much of this debate has been its emotional temperature rather than its factual content. If the move to simplified formulae is not to intensify these arguments, then a careful examination of the formulae must be undertaken and decisions about shifting of funding made on a factual basis.

The funding of special needs has similarly attracted a great deal of emotional debate and, with increased pressures to delegate special needs funding, enormous care will have to be taken in devising the criteria for delegation. This chapter will explore how one LEA has attempted to deal with these two emotive issues.

The teaching staff cost element and the AWPU

The changes in AWPUs, as pupils move from a junior school to a secondary school, are considerable. According to the CIPFA statistics for 1992, the averages for all counties were £882 and £1,254 for pupils in Years 6 and 7 respectively. These figures are, however, in line with SSA figures in which funding for 5 to 11 is weighted 0.7 compared with a weighting of 1 for 11- to 16-year-olds. It can be calculated that 0.7 of £1,254 is £877.80. However, in Cumbria, as in most LEAs, a mythology grew up round such figures that:

- changes in pupils during a six-week period in one summer could not justify such a dramatic difference;

- secondary schools were generously funded;
- Cumbria primary schools fared badly nationally;

and that, therefore, there was an irresistible case for shifting funding from secondary to primary schools.

It was against this background that the committee reviewing Cumbria's LMS scheme asked a group of primary and secondary heads to draw up a set of recommendations for the funding of the teaching staff element of the AWPU 'within the existing resources'.

Prompted by being set this task, the group members searched for evidence which would provide a factual basis for the work. These were some of the figures they came up with:

(1)   a national differential of 11 per cent between average salaries of primary and secondary teachers due largely to a salary structure imposed by statute (ref. Fourth Report of the interim Advisory Committee on Schoolteachers' Pay and Conditions, January 1991, Table 20);

(2)   class contact ratios in 1990 were 0.995 and 0.744 in primary and secondary schools respectively (ref. Schoolteachers' Review Body, First Report, 1992, Table 9);

(3)   that, in a comparison between Cumbria's family group of LEAs and all LEAs nationally, Cumbria turned out to be relatively more generous to its primary schools compared with lower secondary;

(4)   in a comparison of AWPUs in the ten northern authorities, Cumbria ranked sixth for primary schools and came tenth for secondary schools;

(5)   in a report by the Cumbria County Treasurer to the Education Committee in October 1992 it emerged that the schools had balances of £4,000,000 of a total budget of £115,000,000 with primary schools carrying forward nearly twice the percentage of their budgets compared with secondary schools.

There had been widespread talk of secondary schools being the 'fat cats' of the system. Among the many conclusions to be drawn from these figures were:

- nearly a quarter of secondary schools ended the year in deficit, whilst only an eighth of primary schools had deficits;
- 75 per cent of the total deficit was held by secondary schools;
- primary schools carried forward percentage net balances almost twice those of secondaries;
- schools spend £5.3 million more on staff than the formula generated. The overspend was most marked in secondary schools where 42 out of 44 schools 'overspent' their staffing allocation. Not surprisingly, overspends were largest in schools where the number of pupils on roll divided by 30 was a little larger than a whole number.

An analysis of the figures given above clearly demonstrates that impressions can be very misleading. Items 1 and 2, when combined, point to a differential in teaching staff costs for the AWPU of more than 31 per cent. If this is then combined with the differences in average class sizes between primary and secondary, a difference of beween 35 and 40 per cent in teaching costs is indicated.

Understandably the primary sector can argue that the funding simply reflected contact ratios and class sizes current at the time LMS was introduced and that these should be adjusted to take account of the new realities of the National Curriculum, the need for non-contact time, etc.

The work of the group

The group agreed that the innovations of the last five years had placed similar demands for time on both primary and secondary schools. In formulating a rationale for the calculation of teaching staff costs, the assumptions set out below were agreed and applied equally to primary and secondary:

(1) Maximum teaching group size of 30 with the following exceptions:
    (a) reception class – maximum 26;
    (b) Science in specialist labs, Years 7 to 11 – maximum 25;
    (c) Technology in specialist rooms, Years 7 to 11 – maximum 20.
(2) In order to provide specialist support teaching in Years 5 and 6, an addition of one teacher for one day per week for each class of 30 pupils.
(3) Additional staffing be provided for differentiation in years 10 and 11.
(4) A contact ratio of 0.8 for all schools in line with the figure currently used in most secondary schools during curriculum planning.

Examples of the calculations carried out to establish a teacher entitlement are given in Appendices 5.1 and 5.2. The calculation led to an entitlement of

Table 5.1. Teacher entitlement for a secondary pupil in different sizes

	Entitlement	
Year group size	Years 7, 8 and 9	Years 10 and 11
40– 70	0.058	0.073
70–100	0.054	0.066
100–130	0.052	0.064
130–160	0.052	0.064
160–190	0.050	0.063
190–220	0.051	0.063
220–250	0.051	0.063
250–280	0.051	0.063

This further complication had produced a highly charged atmosphere in which debate and the evolution of policy continue albeit in an atmosphere of suspicion and cynicism. The attempt to produce a scheme for special educational needs which was to be 'demand led but cash limited' has given Cumbria an extremely complicated educational policy knot to untie.

Simplification of formulae

One suspects that the Secretary of State's desire to see funding formulae simplified is not educationally driven. If funding formulae are to reflect real needs experienced by those delivering education, they must be composed of a large number of parts which may well move differentially with time. 'Broadbrush' treatments are likely to lead to less informed judgements and may rely more on emotion and mythology than on objective criteria. No doubt a simplified funding formula would ease the move to financing by a Funding Agency. The elaborate formulae and Byzantine calculations, which produce the standard spending assessments, are not, perhaps, a model for LMS formulae. However, by concentrating attention on all the costs involved in delivering education, LMS formulae keep open a route for arguing for adequate resources. Even if simplification is imposed by statute, LEAs teachers' associations and governor groups would be well advised to maintain notional funding formulae if for no better reason than that they will be able to demonstrate objectively the real gap between funds available and funds needed.

Appendix 5.1

The staffing model

For primary schools the calculations are based on the maximum class sizes given in the text above and are as follows:

Year	Reception	Years 1, 2, 3, 4	Years 5, 6
Maximum class size	26	30	30
Additional staffing	0	0	0.2
Total staffing	1	1	1.2
Teachers required	1.25	1.25	1.5
Entitlement	*0.048*	*0.042*	*0.050*

For secondary schools similar calculations have been carried out. Because of the generally larger size of the schools concerned these figures have been calculated in year group sizes and the average figures taken (see Appendix 5.2).

Below are some worked examples of staffing entitlements for various primary-phase schools. Appendix 5.2 does the same for secondary schools.

Worked examples in the primary sector

('Current' means allocation on current staffing model, 'incr.' means approximate increase due to applying model.)

Small primary school, no. on roll 56, 8/yr group

R	0.384	
1–4	1.344	
5/6	0.800	current incr.
	2.528	(2.256, ~ 0.3)

Medium-sized primary school, no. on roll 140, 20/yr group

R	0.96	
1–4	3.36	
5/6	2.00	current incr.
	6.32	(5.64, ~ 0.7)

Junior school, no. on roll 260, 65/yr group

3/4	5.46	
5/6	6.50	current incr.
	11.96	(10.4, ~ 1.56)

Infant school, no. on roll 180, 60/yr group

R	2.88	
1/2	5.04	current incr.
	7.92	(7.32, ~ 0.6)

For the smallest year groups these arrangements do not satisfy the National Curriculum requirements for History and Geography whilst allowing GCSE courses in Technology, a second foreign language, or Music and Art. This extra requirement has been built into the following figures, affecting year groups of 60 and below:

Years 10 and 11:

Size of year group	Number of teacher periods	Entitlement
40	96	0.075
50	126	0.079
60	126	0.066
70	158	0.071
80	158	0.062
90	196	0.068
100	198	0.062
110	236	0.067
120	236	0.061
130	276	0.066
140	276	0.062
150	314	0.065
160	316	0.062
170	354	0.065
180	354	0.061
190	394	0.065
200	394	0.062
210	432	0.064
220	434	0.062
230	472	0.064
240	472	0.061
250	512	0.064
260	512	0.062
270	550	0.064
280	552	0.062
Overall average		0.064

The average for year groups between 70 and 180 is also 0.064.

CHAPTER 6

Appraisal – variations on a theme: one headteacher's stream of consciousness

ED McCONNELL

Although the introduction of teacher appraisal in schools was fore-shadowed in the Education Acts of 1986 and 1988 it became a formal requirement as from September 1992. However, within the new context of self-managing schools, Ed McConnell argues for a fundamentally different purpose of the processes of performance appraisal. As a result of recent experience, he asserts that performance appraisal should not be conceived as a hierarchical control or an accountability mechanism. Rather, appraisal should be part of the process of school self-review. It should be a compass that points towards constancy in a shared value system for the school and provides clear direction in planning and evaluative processes for the continuous development of exemplary professional conduct by individuals as members of teams. Thus, performance appraisal offers a new focus for development planning with an emphasis on collective achievement, through the work of individuals within teams. These are the teachers who implement the plans and achieve the objectives agreed within a full sense of collegial purpose in self-managing schools.

In mid-1994 appraisal cannot be said to have yet had a fundamental influence on the way schools work. This is certainly the case at The Marlborough School. What can be described, however, is the way in which appraisal, in one school at least, is beginning to act as a way of interpreting all the different influences and constraints bearing in on schools in the late twentieth century.

In judging the present in this one school I felt impelled to look back, in very general terms at least, at past experience – both my own and that of the school – to try to anchor the development of appraisal in a historical context. Having always had a strong belief in the concept of appraisal, I have been worried that now that it is here, I do not feel quite so eager to implement it.

My worry has nothing to do with time, energy or money, but it is about the very real tension between individual self-review and whole-school review. We have, for all sorts of readily discovered historical reasons, approached the former via the latter, and maybe that has been the wrong way around? Have we, perhaps, somehow reached our present level of understanding of school effectiveness and how to maintain it, by missing out a step?

Strictly speaking, I do not now, I confess, believe too strongly in the appraisal of individuals. Twenty-five years ago I would have accepted it as a necessary development in a process leading towards a better-led, better-managed teaching force comfortably operating in more confidently organized schools. The importance of appraisal then would have been that it would have had even more to do with its influence on the appraisers, rather than the appraisees, than is now the case. It would have made senior teachers, as they appraised others, consider their own practice; it would have tested their certainties and assumptions enabling them to work out for themselves to whom they were accountable. More particularly they would have discovered more readily what their real responsibilities actually were.

Amongst their real responsibilities, as I saw them then from the perspective of a junior teacher, would have been a commitment to developing the organization of the school in order to maximize the potential of all the staff – whether teacher or not. That was not, however, the approach. Emphasis was placed instead upon replicating forms of organization designed to control – whether that be control of teachers, pupils or parents. That emphasis is no longer current. Those who manage schools are a lot less guilty of not knowing where they are going, and they know to whom they are accountable. There is more taste for change, more desire for a truer understanding of how children learn, than could have been witnessed even fifteen years ago. Most interestingly, the development of recording of achievement for children arising, in turn, from the movement toward whole-school evaluation in the late 1970s, may have been the most significant influence on senior managers in schools. What that sort of influence has yet to unravel is the 'mystery' of how school organization can be adapted to bring about lasting improvement in how children learn.

Nonetheless, it can be argued that the child-centred approach of the 1960s and 1970s, presently so discredited in ministerial rhetoric, may have been the reason why teacher appraisal has become a 'missing link'. Teachers may, in fact, have instituted their own appraisal some time ago through their concern to know more about how children learn. In the process they may have lost control of their 'action research', thus presenting too often an image of what they were doing which lacked clarity and substance. Formal appraisal, because it concentrates on what the teacher, rather than the child, is doing, has to be useful in restoring the balance between an understanding of teaching in relation to learning. My worry is that it will swing the pendulum too far away from more imaginative developments in school organization. However, we can make sure, simply by being aware of that pitfall, that that does not happen, and that appraisal will take its place as the underpinning influence on school organization – an influence which keeps classrooms actively in sharp focus. At The Marlborough School we have meant by that a constant questioning about how children are to be organized for teaching purposes, and about how teachers are to organize themselves in teams to be most effective in communicating with each other and with children.

Appraisal, in bestowing on the appraisee-teacher the right to 'answer back' which children, through recording of achievement, have enjoyed for some while, opens up new opportunities for dialogue. Confused though it is, as presently constructed in the government scheme, based so squarely as a system upon the ultra-hierarchical model of school organization, it remains the best starting point schools may ever have had for opening up the real debate about how they are organized. Teachers are now in a position to question the assumptions upon which school organization is based. It can be argued that they are under a duty to present such a challenge. Senior teachers, confident in their knowledge and interested in debate, are more likely to see such calling to account as a healthy tension which will aid educational advance.

Many commentators, of course, have seen delegation of funds – local management of schools – as the key challenge to the old order. New cost centres would be created, first tackling inefficiency. Savings would be channelled into more teachers, more technical support, a better learning environment. An awareness of performance indicators, short-term targets, longer-term objectives and stated aims would affect, for the better, the performance of all teachers and those charged with managing them.

A nationally imposed curriculum framework and assessment system, coupled with an exponential increase in the quantity of information to be culled from schools, was to complete the set of levers necessary to produce a longed-for educational ideal. But not quite. Initial teacher-training needed attention, too. Making that school-based would shorten the distance between current classroom practitioners and teacher-trainers too far removed from the real experience of children.

Successive Secretaries of State blew warm, then cold, then hot on appraisal. It was seen as yet another lever which, when pulled, would dramatically alter teachers' attitudes and performance, whilst also improving the managerial capability of headteachers and deputies. Implementation of the government appraisal scheme, it needs to be remembered, has coincided with the first three full years of LMS; the arrival of OFSTED and the first inspections under its new framework; comparative tables of examination results; an attempt at the first reported National Curriculum Tests at Key Stage 3; and the Education Act 1993 designed to produce legislation to weaken further local authority control of schools. These are the same local authorities which have become 'the appraising body' for their own schools; which have been given enhanced powers to deal with 'failing' schools; and which are to retain the fullest possible responsibility for special educational needs.

Legislation redefining governors' powers – the same 1986 Act which gave powers to introduce appraisal – and that concerning teachers' pay and imperatives for management which come from the cycle of discussion, under-taken by the team, to set up, implement and evaluate plans of action. Thus, senior management cannot get too closely involved in the definition of jobs down the line. To do so would contradict the validity of any attempt made to push responsibility downwards.

Naturally, the school's development planning process had to be seen as the way to relate objectives for team leaders to the explicit aims of the school. Yet this process, as we discovered, could barely be started in earnest until a great deal of learning about people had been done. I had to understand the nature of those closest to me – deputies and senior teachers. They, in turn, needed to acknowledge their trust in me. Teachers had to be given time to explore each other's ideas in an open and honest way. Their trust in each other is likely always to be the most important element.

Other audiences, too, to which the school was playing needed to be under-stood. Getting to this level of communication was not achieved by one person stating some self-generated explicit aims as the basis for discussion. Only when the agendas of the different interest groups – pupils, parents, teachers, governors, LEA, the community, the public – had been matched could genuine development planning take place. In our experience, therefore, this took five years.

Part of the process of matching agendas was in-service training for our teachers, targeted on appraisal. This was taking place coincidentally as appraisal schemes were being piloted in a number of local authorities. The approach was oblique. Going back to basics seemed right. We unravelled together the complexities of school organization – the basis of our organization of pupils, our curriculum design, our reporting to parents, our reporting to governors. 'Audience' became the 'buzz word'. The implications of the then impending LMS were added into the equation.

Out of that training came a unanimous view from staff that they wanted a triangular peer appraisal approach based upon an inter-visitation model between faculties. They clamoured for clearer definition of the purposes behind their work, but through their interaction with each other, not through an unwieldly managerial approach. By the time Kenneth Clarke announced the definite introduction of appraisal in December 1990 (in a press release entitled 'Teacher Appraisal to be Compulsory'), they had gone a long way towards understanding that assurance of quality in the classroom could only happen at their level because it was their responsibility and no one else's. The Secretary of State's emphasis on quality control, that is the assurance of min-imum quality, in telling teachers that they would, 'soon become accustomed to having their work appraised by senior staff in a way that many people in other occupations find quite familiar' had quite a hollow ring, particularly when he was at pains to explain that he would not find sufficient money to implement his scheme on the basis of the National Steering Group's recom-mendation. Teachers were not, of course, rejecting individual professional development, rather they were recognizing the role of others in their development. This understanding was also crucial in clearing out of the way any misconceived notions about performance-related pay.

Governors had readily involved themselves in a similar training process to that of the staff, but a year earlier. The philosophical, social-psychological, historical and political roots of the development of the school to that date were closely examined. Shared values had hitherto been assumed; they needed some clearer articulation. Appraisal was not to be the governors' direct business and they had to be able to understand why. We concerned ourselves, therefore, with the process of explaining the positive nature of their role to enable them to sanction more readily the plans presented to them. The school's scheme for appraisal would be one amongst many plans for managing the development of the school.

Involving governors and staff in fundamental discussion had its benefits. Some of those benefits disappeared, however, as governor turnover took place. Keeping track of who had discussed the issues and who had not was difficult. Teaching staff change too; so do the various audiences. The one constant was the headteacher. There came a point when I found this responsibility to be particularly burdensome.

A headteacher's personal vision for a school inevitably influences processes of planning as well as outcomes. The reality of development planning is that it is in the hands of the headteacher. My main point of contact with classroom teachers had to be through heads of faculty. To say that the matching of different agendas was a matter of chance – desired and prayed for, but not managed – would be a denial of the truth. Contact with governors is spasmodic and, when it happens, much business is still conducted through the medium of retrospective report as events overtake plans with a relentless dynamism. The 'fruit machine' analogy gives way to a comparison with the footballer who is not given time to settle on the ball. Headteachers have had that problem of late, but so have those around them, namely, governors, teachers and parents.

The potential for confusion and overload in the minds of these groups has been very great indeed, allowing a greater than usual opportunity for headteachers to be very directive. This was the burden for me, becoming almost a matter of conscience. The climate of appraisal ought to be about the empowerment of others, as I have described. This was not how it felt.

My anxiety about steering others so deliberately coincided with my own appraisal. Conscious of my own unique powers to determine the way in which the school was to develop, I chose to concentrate in my own appraisal upon the way in which I had managed, over five or so years, the 'matching of the different agendas' but with a particular focus on the staff of the school. My concern was that I had 'clouted in' too much change, worked teachers too hard and, in short, given more consideration to my own agenda than anybody else's.

My resolve to bare my soul in this way was strengthened by my participation in a scheme for school self-evaluation over the period 1988–92. This scheme, an extension of the then current practice in Oxfordshire, had been designed to become a model for whole-school support integrated into a model for

- Appraisal empowers appraisees to challenge in a way not experienced hitherto. Managing this energy is not easy.

- Maintaining the interest of teachers in any kind of planning – whether they be those in senior/middle management positions or those who belong to the dwindling ranks of the 'ordinary' classroom teacher – is not easy.

- Falling rolls in the late 1980s made an open appointments system well-nigh impossible; rising rolls at a time of severe budget stringency are having the same effect. This can be a major constraint on staff development.

- Staff development policies may have raised individual expectations without creating a full understanding, as yet, of the responsibility the beneficiaries have towards the school.

- National Curriculum assessment arrangements may still continue to have a crucial effect on the professional liberty of teachers.

- Time to get started on appraisal for all has not been easy to find. Money delegated to support appraisal coincided with cuts in funding.

I stress the term 'background issues and problems' which I used above. They are not all of equal weight or mutually exclusive and the list is not exhaustive. It signifies potential pitfalls which one needs to acknowledge openly in order to avoid complacency. It does not represent, and has not represented, real issues and problems which are having to be faced at all times; it is meant, rather, to qualify the reader's understanding of the following account of the practicalities of setting up an appraisal scheme at The Marlborough School.

In common with the majority of schools, The Marlborough approached appraisal in the initial stages by setting up a working group. A deliberate decision was taken to make this group as broadly based as possible, regardless of size. Eight people were sufficient, ultimately, to form the group, covering the interests of four teacher unions, heads of faculties, subject leaders, senior tutors, newly qualified teachers, year tutors, subject teachers, part-time teachers and the most senior teachers. Logically the professional tutor, also the Deputy Head, chaired the group. As Headteacher I consciously distanced myself from the whole exercise. First, I was involved in my own appraisal and that of a peer in another school at the same time; second, I was aware of the potential difficulty of having to arbitrate over aspects of the system to be adopted and the pairings chosen.

The working group stressed four main issues when proposing an outline scheme to colleagues:

- the lack of peer appraisal/observation in the government scheme and opportunities for using such evidence;

- the importance of using appraisal as part of a team-building process;
- the need for confidentiality; and
- the care required in co-ordinating and timing the whole process.

Generally, the group's reaction was positive, and reconciling the statutory requirements with staff needs was not seen as an insurmountable task. The potential of the appraisal process in stimulating individual staff development was applauded, but the use of the already well-constructed teams as the basis of the pairings was seen as supportive of collective development. Membership of more than one team was also seen as useful rather than too complex for the flexibility it offered in creating satisfactory pairings. One of the more important recommendations made was that the information-gathering element of the appraisal cycle should be widened to include observation and comment by peers. Thus, five main recommendations emerged, reflecting most of the debate of the group, but also advice culled from the Oxfordshire Framework for Teacher and Headteacher Appraisal of 1991 and Circular 12/91 itself:

(1) Appraisal pairings were to be based on a team approach reflecting the working practices in the school. Six major areas of team activity were identified – the senior staff, the faculties, administration, counselling and guidance, post-16 education and community education.

(2) The information-gathering aspect of the appraisal cycle had to be widened to admit evidence from peers.

(3) The time-span covering the process was not to exceed eight working weeks.

(4) A named member of staff was to have responsibility for co-ordinating and managing the scheme.

(5) A *complete* confidentiality rule was to be observed at all times.

A further recommendation made referred to the training needs of staff with interviewing and classroom observation skills being given top priority. It was also emphasized that all training should be delivered to members of the same team at the same time to avoid mixed messages.

This latter recommendation, more than any other, pointed up the level of trust staff had in each other as they approached appraisal. They had to make the scheme their own in the fullest sense. If earlier decisions about managing the school had meant anything in practice – that is 'people in the middle being given genuine responsibility to manage, and a proper opportunity to exercise powers of leadership' – then the ownership of appraisal had to rest firmly with all. Simple involvement of staff in discussion, on the basis of a pre-set plan, would not have been enough. The most senior teachers had to stand away, in a definite show of disinterest, if only to give substance to the notion that appraisal is potentially a great leveller, but in the most constructive sense. This is the teacher's 'right to answer back' in a spirit of true debate with senior colleagues. That debate at The Marlborough happily produced live consequences which took us back to our agreed positions in the summer of 1988, interpreting for us the true nature of appraisal.

Appraisal, we are beginning to discover, tests the values of the school; it insists on development planning and a programme for staff development which is utterly explicit. More than anything else it requires a code of professional conduct from which there is no escape for any individual, regardless of status. Once a system of appraisal is in place, it becomes clear that it is appraisal which determines the need for shared values, sound planning and exemplary professional conduct; it is not the other way round.

At The Marlborough the building of the school's approach to appraisal has begun to highlight more sharply that development planning is not a pencil and paper exercise revolving around a prescribed model; nor is it a process which happens as a result of a laid-down structure of meetings relentlessly reporting up or down the hierarchy. Models tend to give equal weighting to each stage of planning, seeming also to suggest that the earlier stages are actually in the control of those running the school. In reality the historical position is always the starting point, and no amount of auditing or rewriting of the script can alter that. Similarly, what can be called the 'stop the world I want to get off' approach, which implies that specific periods of time can be allocated in advance for reaching a target, is rarely reasonable. The variable responses of people day to day render such accuracy impossible. Evaluation, therefore, we have found, deserves the greatest weighting in the planning process because it is evaluation which keeps people talking with each other and thinking coherently about what they are doing. There is, again as we have learned through experience, a crucial link between evaluation and appraisal which needs to be made. Individuals need to understand the responsibility they have to gain an intellectual grasp of the aims and objectives of the school and to maintain themselves in a state of constant self-review in relation to those aims and objectives. It is this understanding which yields that assurance of quality which cannot be gained by a chain reaction down the line. Teachers do not find this easy to follow, but governors may be even further away from a clear view of what it all may mean.

In reporting to governors on the issue of appraisal we have found that their understanding of their role has been somewhat hazy. Many have found it difficult to distinguish between a responsibility to ensure an appraisal scheme is in place and for monitoring its progress, and the right to be involved in judgements on individual teacher performance. Some, certainly, had appraisal linked in their minds to performance-related pay and disciplinary matters. For the most part they were too polite to engage in much challenging debate and they accepted the very thorough briefing they were given as the basis of their decision to endorse the scheme prepared by the staff. Nonetheless, the lingering doubt remains that the correct connections are being made in their minds between the school's aims, development planning, the roles different teachers are asked to play, classroom management and the assurance of quality. Circular

12/91 suggests that governors should be privy to a summary of the targets set for appraisees and that they should be informed of the progress made in reaching those targets. The worry has to be that such reporting could come outside the context of whole-school development given the different time-scales over which evaluation, inspection, appraisal and development planning take place. Governing bodies, too, last just four years.

We must reserve judgement about the actual experience of teacher appraisal at The Marlborough School. Insufficient time has elapsed to enable data to be logged and an adequate record to be compiled. What is known, however, is that appraisal may hold the key to a more collective understanding of how the school may develop through constant self-review and a more open understanding of the relationship between teachers. However, some caveats can be stated.

My reliance upon team review depends very heavily upon strong line man-agement insisting upon detailed day-to-day monitoring of events. In short, self-evaluation, at whatever level in the organization, has to be managed. It is not a technique which cuts out management. Individual failure, fatigue, boredom, recalcitrance, and more besides, will always be there and will always need to be dealt with. These are matters of discipline which cannot be confused with longer-term planning for an individual's personal and professional develop-ment. Let us assume, however, that we can get the balance right.

Seen as an unthreatening exploration of values, ideas, processes, systems and outcomes, appraisal becomes a centrally important tool in school leader-ship and management which defines what we do and the way we do it. I have to warn, however, that its usefulness is diminished considerably if it is seen as a way of testing what we do and the way we do it. Conversely, it is also clear to me that, at the level of the individual – and ironically given government intentions in introducing appraisal – it may become increasingly difficult for headteachers and those with delegated management powers to deal adequately with poor performance. My own techniques for dealing with poor performance – and the introduction of appraisal has made it clear to me just how frequently and directly in the past I have tackled such matters, that is, surprisingly often and very straightforwardly – have always been a mixture of 'iron fist' and 'velvet glove'. Given that the process of appraisal never stops because of the size of the task, it is impossible to distinguish an in-between period during which the 'normal' reasonably satisfactory management practices of the past can operate. Good relationships, rightly heavily encouraged by appraisal, are enormously important – but not at any price!

In the future, therefore, we would like to see appraisal stimulate change, or, more exactly, the growth of professional confidence, in a number of ways. It is often thought to be fanciful on the part of governors and headteachers that the aims of a school are to be taken seriously, in the sense that there is a direct line between aims and the way individuals working in the school actually conduct themselves. Perhaps appraisal, because it makes shared values so schools gradually transferred resources from local authorities to the schools. The formulation of a National Curriculum was envisaged within this framework of LMS. Further, whilst resources would be available directly to the school, the National Curriculum was to be prescribed in great detail by centralized authorities. Management of the curriculum in this style assumed a top-down approach with all the problems of institutions either understanding or accepting the meanings of a centralized authority. To further compound these matters, the contexts for the delivery of a National Curriculum and site-based management were complicated by the ability of schools to 'opt out' from the local authority and pursue their site-based management in direct relationship to central government.

Unfortunately, the strategies for change and the development of a new infrastructure were not considered in enough depth. The idea and its operation in reality became the victim of particular pressure groups and it began to take on the worst excesses of a partial ideological outlook, as well as alienating professionals from what was considered something worthwhile at its inception in 1988. This has led to an unsystematic attempt at implementing the National Curriculum. It has been a distressing experience in the sense that it could have been an opportunity to gain an understanding of what might be needed for an educational system for the twenty-first century. However, as with all things, some parts might provide ways forward for the future. In the last part of this chapter, I suggest ways forward from the mistakes that have been made, and a possible infrastructure for turning ideas into practice. It would be hoped that an infrastructure of the type proposed might lead to the dialogue and understanding necessary to support schools as self-managing institutions in an educative democracy.

The curriculum had been the focus of educational reports before the 1988 Reform Act. Various HMI publications, especially the so-called 'Red Books', had put forward views based upon their findings from practical inspections and 'dip-stick' operations around the country (DES, 1985b). They identified areas of experience which they felt should be in a curriculum which was broad, balanced, relevant and coherent. Curriculum specialists, experts and teachers were well aware of the possibilities of a common, cultural curriculum arising from the practice of schooling, the development of students' learning and philosophic reasons. Certainly other types of curriculum were posited which saw subjects not as ends in themselves, but rather as means to an end. For many years project work, interrelated and integrated studies were well founded, particularly in primary schools. The teaching of basic skills of numeracy and literacy was not neglected and most HMI reports suggested that teachers use a variety of approaches in the gaining of these skills (Bolton, 1992). Assessment practices were beginning to take on new directions, both with the work of the Assessment and Performance Unit (APU) and inroads into the collecting of portfolios of children's work and the concept of Records of Achievement.

The 1988 Education Reform Act, as stated at the beginning of this chapter, consisted of two very different concerns, both of which had a strong impact on each other. The two parts were to produce tensions which meant that a coherent policy was extremely difficult to operate. In one section of the Act there were the requirements for the National Curriculum and the possible assessment arrangements. The second part of the Act had more to do with how schools were to be managed, in a context where local government account-ability and control was being diminished and national control of education was being enhanced. In particular, this second part was to lay the foundation for LMS, the setting up of grant-maintained (GM) schools, open admissions to schools and a language and conceptual base which owed much to a market economy view of the education system. This second part was then to be further amplified in the Education Bill of 1993. These two parts to the Act fundamentally meant that in practice it would be very difficult for a coherent curriculum policy to be worked out. The aims of the Education Reform Act of 1988, in terms of what it was trying to do, assume shared cultural perceptions which are undermined by its second part. In terms of the enactment of policy, issues concerning the features of LMS proved to be a time-consuming focus for school leaders. At the same time, the National Curriculum was extending teachers, with incredible burdens of working out new curricula, in which they had very little input. The curriculum problem was further compounded because there was no overall view of the purposes of the curriculum except in terms of subjects. Once the subject teams had been set up, each one would quite naturally stress the full dimensions and scope of its territory. Subjects may or may not have domains of learning in terms of concepts and skills which are *sui generis*, but historically many of them have arisen because they are culturally valued activities whose content has travelled far and wide, often subsuming other areas of knowledge. Often the focus for certain subjects, especially practical ones like technology or physical education, includes the uses and practice of many aspects of other disciplines.

The actual purposes of the 1988 Act are probably ones which most people feel they could adhere to. They are:

(1) To promote the spiritual, moral, cultural, mental and physical development of pupils of the school and of society.
(2) To prepare such pupils for the opportunities, responsibilities and experiences of adult life.

These two aims denote the two main purposes of an initiation into a curriculum whch prepares students for social, economic and personal roles in future society. And the other aim prepares students for membership of a demo-cratic society. An analysis of such matters will probably lead us to ask what sort of general educational aims our democratic values actually generate. First, they seem to occur around some idea of the development of the individual, in particular the development of one's identity within that society. By building self-esteem and self-respect the young student becomes stronger in hope and confidence which gives him/her the ability to feel empowered, and a feeling of forming a view of the world by interacting with its natural and social government, by control of a national testing system, systems of opting out of local control and constraining spending allowances to local authorities, could bypass local democracy. The point is that if you wish to have control at the point of production in terms of institutions, then that has to be localized. But to have a curriculum and the schools devising things locally would have meant that the purposes of the education in terms of some substantial national priorities could not occur. We know from international studies that the effects of certain testing systems alter fundamentally the ways in which teaching and learning take place in schools. Simplistic, slimmed-down, multiple-choice-type testing produces many problems; for instance, in science, Professor Paul Black has outlined the following:

- science is reduced to the learning of isolated facts and skills;
- the cognitive level of classroom work is lowered;
- pupils have to work at too great a pace for effective learning;
- in particular, ground is 'covered' by a race through a textbook;
- much teaching time is devoted to direct test preparation;
- pupils' questioning is inhibited;
- learning follows testing in focusing on aspects that are easy to test;
- laboratory work stops unless tests include laboratory tests;
- creative, innovative methods and topical content are dropped;
- teachers' autonomy is constrained and their methods revert to a uniform style;
- teachers are led to violate their own standards of good teaching.
                                                              (Black, 1993, p. 52)

There is no doubt that the overall effect of some very anachronistic testing devices, produced particularly at Key Stage 3 in the summer of 1993, was to make the profession realize that they would be pushed back into teaching in a fashion which it was not prepared to undertake. The new GCSE examination which had put much emphasis on continuous assessment and the collection of course-based assignments was once more reviewed. Those with a minimalist view of the curriculum put through new orders on GCSE exams which gave much less credence to course-based assessment and teacher assessment. In effect, the whole issue surrounding the testing became a national issue because teachers could see:

(1)   that these types of tests were constraining the nature of the curriculum activity they wished to implement;

(2)   that teachers would have to teach to the test, with all the worries about constraining the creative elements of learning;

(3)   that the teachers would not have their assessments taken into account in terms of any summative proposals;

(4)   that as the tests were to be taken on certain days, this meant that children could not take them when they were ready for them, or needed them;

(5) that the types of tests which were appearing seemed to disregard notions of capability which the National Curriculum had set out to put forward, so there would be no assessment of the deliberative and reflective qualities of much of a student's work;

(6) that the students would be assessed only in written terms, even though much of their work, if it had been active, may have been achieved orally or on a project basis.

(National Co-ordinating Committee on Learning and Assessment, 1993b)

Further, the tests, despite their claims to reliability if not validity, were going to take place in very different contexts. The contexts were partly formed by those structural changes which have already been mentioned as part of the Education Reform Act of 1988. Certain schools were grant-maintained in status, which meant that they had opted out of local authority control. The implication of opting out was not that these schools escaped the National Curriculum, as they were government controlled, but rather that the differential funding made sure that these schools received double entitlement in terms of financial assistance in certain aspects. It is interesting to note that in a recent survey it was shown that the schools which were able to afford training in a more varied way were those schools which had, indeed, gained monies by being grant-maintained. State schools with the local authority found that their budget could not stretch to many activities and were operating much in-service work themselves. LMS, welcomed by headteachers, in reality amounts to very little space for the redistribution of monies within school. Most of the money is already tied up in terms of staffing, of goods needed to keep the school going, and of services to be provided. There is a myth that great management decisions can be made in terms of the resources of the school. Unfortunately, despite much time being taken up by heads in going on courses to prepare for this decision-making, it has proved to be another Holy Grail. There is very little room for manoeuvre in terms of the money.

In schools site-based management has produced structures for financial administration. Whilst it is true that some of these structures are more ordered than before, the issues discussed and the decisions made are often not different in terms of importance and have often meant administering matters of little consequence. At our own school, the bursar still manages all the accounts, except that there are more of them, and they are computerized. Invoices, which once were dealt with by the local authority, are now dealt with by schools. This has made no difference to the control we have over the money we spend, only that we are engaged in more of the practical operations of invoicing, etc. It does mean that we can make and call for our own contracts on certain minor works to do with the buildings or some new project of a building nature. Whilst we have control over more of these activities in terms partnerships with external agencies such as universities and LEAs was not recognized.

(10) A destructive tension existed between competing ideologies emphasizing a neo-liberal, market-led philosophy allied to traditionalist educational assumptions and a more liberal, humanist perspective which emphasizes more entitlements, rights and shared cultural values.

(11) There was a lack of recognition of the practices of teachers in course-based assessment and the move towards more authentic ways of representing students' learning.

Proposed infrastructure for research and effective learning

From this analysis it can be seen that we need to reconstruct the national system so that dialogue can occur and there can be a renewal of the processes of rational enquiry into educational issues between educationalists, and between educationalists and other stake-holders.

If some of these issues had been realized before the decision to set up a National Curriculum was taken, then it might have been approached in a completely different way. Certainly, it needed an infrastructure which could deliver shared perceptions of changes in the curriculum and schools in a manageable, informed and sensitive way. So what might these areas of consideration have been in setting up the National Curriculum? What sort of infrastructure might be needed? What sorts of practices and research need we be concerned with in making decisions?

Table 7.1 sets out some areas which still need to be considered and I suggest an infrastructure and the areas of research which are being investigated, or need to be investigated, in order to ensure a critical dialogue and illumination of the issues. But this, of course, needs to be within a system with its focus on students' learning and also the informing of national government about the priorities of its education system. Furthermore, if parents and governors are not to be given partial or biased information, they must have the assurance that they will receive well-researched material on which to base decisions. It is essential that the provision for this knowledge base is achieved in conjunction with HE institutions. These are the only places which have the databases and the expertise, the space and the time, to provide these services. Interaction at all levels between HE institutions and schools is an imperative of strong dimensions for future planning.

From these considerations it seems that we need an infrastructure which really does have impact upon the way in which students learn, their performance and the improvement in terms of what and how they learn. If we are to prepare ourselves for the challenge of a more highly skilled workbase and the

Table 7.1

Areas for consideration	Structure	Research
Curriculum overview of learning needs 3–21, without which no meaningful sense can be made of issues of progression and continuity in the education system.	A National Curriculum Committee with remit to review types of understandings necessary and worthwhile to bring about purposes of education.	How do children gain understanding of the world from an early age? Particularly building on the work of the development of intuitive theories pre-7 and ways in which systematic thought is gained by students until the age of 20.
Understandings of how the curriculum fits into the patterns of lifelong learning.	Committee to investigate ways in which higher education, or companies, or community projects can aid this process.	Research into the skills diminished or enhanced by ageing, notion of work and issues concerning the Third Age.
Issues concerned with the different ways in which pupils learn and the different strategies for learning.	Clusters of schools with HE/LEA with brief to look at this question.	To address the research work on ways of learning. Particularly in recent years the variety of methods, be they of a negotiable or interactive nature, as well as the evidence about innovations such as peer tutoring. To look at these methodologies of learning in terms of their weighting at different ages.
Institutional practices to investigate the whole area of what is meant by school effectiveness and improvement. The relationship of value added in the compilation of any instrument for recording school effectiveness.	Clusters of schools with HE/LEA investigating all these issues.	To look at the latest research of a quantifiable nature in this area as well as the more important and highly developed work coming on line on school improvement, the values involved in this and the multi-levelled plethora of factors involved in influencing environments for improvement.
To look at the issues of building culture and change in schools.	To use again the school clusters and HE/LEA.	To look again at the international research work which indicates the factors involved in successful change. Particularly the need for holistic institutional research and the ways in which cultures are affected by certain organizational patterns and institutional values.

table continues

Areas for consideration	Structure	Research
To provide opportunities for the appropriate and effective training of teachers as something throughout their professional career.	Schools, with HE/LEA working out policies to help build schools as learning communities by a mixture of in-service and accredited courses. It would include ITT, induction programmes and further career development.	Research on the development of teachers and their perceptions and problems in the areas of personal, professional and institutional development.
To set up a system of reviewing the school in partnership with parents and governors for the benefit of students.	Two meetings with parents per year, which includes: (1) a review of progress; (2) action planning about ways forward. Parents and students would be invited in to discuss the record of achievement of the student on the same system as we make dental appointments etc. Hence there is time given during the day for this important matter. It should not be an added extra.	Research in local organizational structures, e.g. Scottish system of assessment, reporting of standards of students and schools.
The timing of assessment. Assessment should be embedded in the learning process and not be a bolt-on activity. Any assessment in controlled conditions should be held by the teacher for the student when thought appropriate.	Teacher in-service work with HE/LEA.	Research on the collection of evidence and data for building a picture of a student in other ways than simple tests, e.g. Record of Achievement, portfolios, etc.
Assessment instruments at regional or national level. The school clusters should have access to materials that provide examples of good assessment practice and may be used as exemplars in terms of methodology of assessing students.	Agency to collect and collate materials which are then recycled to regional centres.	Research along the lines of APU and other learning/ assessment centres.
Standards of assessment instruments for teacher use in schools.	Moderated and trialled materials to be shared as conscience-raising and judgemental experiences for teachers.	Research on ways in which judgements are formed about the qualitative nature of work.

table continues

Areas for consideration	Structure	Research
Continuity and progression in the curriculum areas could be enhanced by progressive instruments, such as the ten-level scale, acting as guidelines over time.	Collaboration between schools/HE/LEA. Ideas and problems discussed between teachers in terms of: (1) What are the features of a progressive nature in the learning? (2) How far skills, concepts, ideas, etc. have to be extended or may be regained or revisited in terms of some learning. (3) What and why certain parts of learning may be regarded as simple tasks and others as more complex.	Research into attainment targets which are criterion referenced but do not relate to factually based material, but can provide some idea of progression and continuity throughout the years of formal education.
Curriculum content. The content of the curriculum should be looked at within the general framework as outlined by the national review of the curriculum, but content left very much to individual schools to decide.	National committee to outline main areas of concepts, skills and dispositions which might be appropriate in the curriculum areas, but these are non-statutory.	Research into what it means both to understand and what understandings are important in fulfilling the purposes of the curriculum.

contingencies of the social changes which will follow in the wake of new forms of working, then it seems that this sort of approach is a possible way forward. It will have a focus, as has been said, on students' learning, but also on the gaining of information which can inform national policy so that enabling frameworks can be set up for the fulfilment of these goals. However, in determining the focus, it also has to be embedded in the practices and interactions of people engaged directly with students and those who can support those practices. I would postulate that we need structures which really enable informed action to take place. Therefore, there must be relevant information available in making decisions and policy structures for the discussion of that data, both in terms of the reality of day-to-day life in schools, and the more generalized observations or, indeed, detailed case-studies of those who have a remit for that purpose.

The proposed infrastructure outlined in Figure 7.1 shows two major foci: one, the learning of students, and two, the making of priorities by national government. The creative and imaginative processes of how students learn, construct and reconstruct the world is made in a local setting. Agencies and groups are there to support, clarify, review and forward that aim. The structures are there for action to take place, hopefully not for its own sake but rather after experiences have been critically reflected upon.

The support structures at a national level will inform both the local context and also the Secretary of State for Education. They have a wide brief to collate,

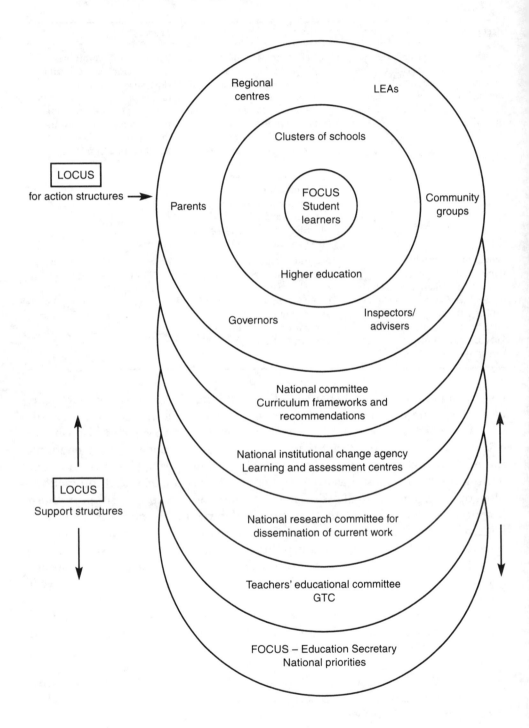

Figure 7.1. A possible national infrastructure. (Source: *A Reconstructed National System, Partnerships for the 21st Century*, NCCLA, March 1993)

synthesize and analyse areas which have direct impact in the workings of schools. They can produce insights, carry out research, act as catalysts and produce frameworks of entitlements; many of these will be foundations or will be university-based, which will hopefuly give them the independence or disinterestedness to advise in as fair a way as possible. Set in place would be the interactions necessary for an educative democratic community. It would be hoped that government initiatives on education would be more driven by a concern for an education which is not ideologically biased in an extremely partial way.

As such, the content in a detailed way will be in the hands of teachers, in consultation with parents, governors, LEAs, regional groups, etc. The information and frameworks for the delivery of an effective learning environment will be made possible by the support structures and networks, whose deliberations can feed directly into their local decision-making. It, hopefully, will enable particular circumstances to be taken into account, yet not be so particular that knowledge and understanding is not seen as something that has much wider currency than the immediate. The searching for a better truth is not that of the solitary figure, but rather that of one who works in conjunction with others to forward the quality of the human condition. This type of structure also allows the very precepts of a conscious, co-operative, democratic liberal culture to proceed.

PART III

Grant-maintained schools and self-managing realities

As outlined in Chapter 1, the establishment of a new publicly funded grant-maintained (GM) sector of schools under the Education Act of 1988, and its subsequent relatively slow growth, has attracted considerable publicity and comment – both favourable and antipathetic.

In this section the heads of two GM schools outline considerations which led to decisions to 'opt out' of their LEAs and seek GM status. Both chapters present case-studies of successful schools – neither under threat of closure (as has been the motivation elsewhere) – where specific local problems and dilemmas were perceived as providing compelling reasons for becoming grant-maintained. For both, perceptions of the importance of providing continuity of high-quality educational opportunities for their pupils through enhanced funding and opportunities for self-managing 'value for money' strategies appear to have been key factors in the pursuit of the objectives of meeting the educational needs of pupils, and the wishes of parents, the communities served and the teaching and support staff.

CHAPTER 8

Burntwood School's transition to GM status: an illustration of the complexities of choice and diversity

BRIGID BEATTIE

Decisions to seek GM status are invariably specific and local – and often based on complex variables of a perceived 'balance of educational advantage'. Brigid Beattie provides specific internal and external considerations which led to the decision to opt for GM status for Burntwood School. In 1992, following achievement of the new status, she describes the ways in which the school established the varied and required detailed mechanisms for successful self-management as a girls' comprehensive school. However, the original decision to become a GM girls' comprehensive school was partially set aside by the LEA's decision in 1993 to introduce a selective entry to its sole boys-only school. Ironically, and to avoid future problems under equal opportunities legislation, Burntwood School is due to receive a selective intake of girls in September 1995; 90 girls out of 280 will be admitted through selective entry.

Burntwood, a girls' comprehensive school, is situated within the inner urban borough of Wandsworth, the Conservatives' 'jewel in the crown' of well-managed boroughs. On the demise of the Inner London Education Authority (ILEA) in 1990 Wandsworth inherited responsibility for running education. The school has 1500 students aged 11 to 18.

Burntwood pupils are typical of those of many inner-London schools. The majority of the pupils (80 per cent) come from local Wandsworth primary schools, the school drawing from over sixty primary schools in total. The intake is diverse, with 70 per cent of the pupils coming from ethnic minority groups. A large proportion of pupils come from socially disadvantaged backgrounds, with over one-third of the intake being entitled to a free school meal and 40 per cent speaking a language other than, or in addition to, English at home. Burntwood pupils' average reading and abstract reasoning scores were at the

Wandsworth average, but with a significantly lower mathematics score, as would be expected in a girls-only intake. HMI, in 1990, stated that: 'The school takes about half of its pupils from economically disadvantaged areas and the remainder from areas described as neither prosperous nor economically disadvantaged' (DES, 1990a). The school is oversubscribed. Examination results, at both 'A' and GCSE levels, are above the national average.

The school possesses a fine site of 13 acres; the buildings date from 1957 and were an award-winning design by the distinguished team of London County Council (LCC) architects. English Heritage has recently applied to the Department for Education (DFE) for listed building status.

Burntwood was founded in September 1986 through the amalgamation of two neighbouring girls' schools as part of the widespread amalgamations programme of the ILEA. The ILEA had been faced with a drastic fall in pupil numbers and met this by amalgamating rather than by closing schools; these amalgamations, with the hindsight of a local management of schools (LMS) focus, look civilized, leisurely and certainly expensive. Pupils attending a school designated for amalgamation were generally allowed to finish their education there. Placements were found in other schools for displaced teachers.

The two schools which were to become Burntwood were very different in ethos. One was in a familiar 1970s tradition: teaching groups organized in mixed-ability sets, a loose, almost non-existent, uniform policy, a pastoral approach to discipline and weak examination results. Pupil numbers dropped dramatically as a large number of pupils moved to another building during asbestos removal. Teaching staff appeared to have developed a 'Dunkirk' spirit which had resulted in an extremely cohesive staffroom. Teaching groups were small, non-contact periods plentiful, opportunities for in-service training good. The contrast of the other school was startling: a strict uniform policy, a banding system for teaching groups, firm discipline and a teaching staff accustomed to authoritarian leadership.

The amalgamation has been acknowledged as one of the most successful in London. Why? Technical reasons meant that the appointment of a new head for the school was delayed for a term. The staff of both schools had an opportunity to play a part, supported by an able advisory headteacher, Rodney Usher, in the drawing up of structures for the school. This process enabled staff to take ownership of the new school in a most positive manner.

The appointment of myself as a head with no connection to either of the parent schools continued the process of cutting away from the past. The Staff Consultative Committee, and indeed other teaching and support staff, through discussion documents, continued to shape the development of the school. Burntwood's structures included cross-curricular working teams and task groups set up to deal with major issues as quickly as possible and to involve both teaching and support staff in the day-to-day management of the school.

> Appointment to the headship of a school to be formed by amalgamating schools is unlike any other headship appointment. It is not a 'green field' situation setting

up a new school nor is it taking over an already established school. It involves bringing together the staffs of two schools and creating a new institution while, at the same time, preserving the educational opportunities for pupils of the contributory schools.

(Richardson, 1988)

The agenda for management of change in the first year of the school, 1986 to 1987, was extraordinary. There were many pressing issues to resolve. We had to translate the aims of the school which had been discussed by governors, staff and pupils into a series of manageable objectives. Staffing structures had to be fleshed out with job descriptions, the ethos defined, models arrived at of curriculum access for all pupils, pastoral structures constructed, a pastoral curriculum drawn up, and the organization of teaching groups resolved. These were key issues to the success and stability of the new school. There were, in addition to these internal changes flowing from the amalgamation, external forces of change which could not be ignored. The year 1986, our amalgamation year, also saw the launch of a new examination – the GCSE. This exam, popular with teachers, also increased their workload and altered teaching practice. Pupils were involved in the shaping of the school. Burntwood has a pupil-designed emblem. The school was rather unimaginatively called Burntwood, by the governors, after the busy road in which it is situated. Pupils had the clever idea of using a burnt tree as our emblem; although the tree appears skeletal it has a rising sun behind it and deep roots below to symbolize opportunity and growth, an extremely appropriate symbol for a girls' school. This logo appears on the school uniform, stationery and flagpole. The next generation of pupils chose a school flower, the red carnation, as a symbol of friendship. Pupils were consulted through their Student Council. We wished to create a school with a strong corporate identity to back the external image.

This process of what would now be called 'marketing the school' was not, in 1986, understood by either staff or governors. Most of the teaching staff and some of the governors were against the adoption of a uniform and ours was a particularly noticeable scarlet! Opinions were voiced that too much of the senior team's time was being spent on image-building, for example, in drawing up a prospectus, in open days and in visiting primary schools. The future of Burntwood was in fact by no means secure. The borough had a surplus of several thousand school places. The amalgamations policy had not been sharp enough.

ILEA had given Burntwood a standard admission number of six forms of entry. This was met in the first year of the school's existence and by the second year the school had become oversubscribed. Burntwood's future, in spite of the negativity of teacher strike action, appeared secure. An inspection by the ILEA Inspectorate in 1988 commented on the school's progress in the following terms:

Burntwood has been fortunate in being able to start its life with a new structure and a new head for this has made planning from first principles easier. From this basis the school has developed and fostered the image of a proactive school which is able to respond positively and coherently to change.

The new school's identity has grown out of the best of each of the 'parent' schools. To have achieved such remarkable success in five terms is a tribute to all involved in the school at every level. With such a sound foundation, it can only move from strength to strength for the benefit of high achievement for all its pupils.

The future appeared secure but outside the school major changes were taking place which were to affect Burntwood.

The unifying philosophy of ILEA had been that of 'educating all London's children'. Teachers felt proud to work in a capital city for the ILEA and its predecessor the LCC. County Hall, on the banks of the Thames, facing the Houses of Parliament, appeared as a visible symbol of the power and security of the Great London Council (GLC) and ILEA. Wherever teachers travelled in the capital there were the familiar green name boards on the authority's vast network of nurseries, schools, FE colleges and adult institutes, and teachers transferred with ease from one institution to another. Cracks were appearing, however, beneath this unity. The authority was criticized for its weak examination results, and its high degree of spending on administration was weakened by the militant teacher action. Its abolition in 1990 appeared a political inevitability.

On 1 April 1990 Burntwood School passed to the management of the borough of Wandsworth. The latter had been the first London borough to wish to leave the ILEA to form its own education authority. Wandsworth combined a sound record of financial and administrative management with a high political profile of the Tory right. Its leader Paul Beresford was to become both a knight and a Member of Parliament.

Wandsworth appointed Donald Naismith, a nationally known figure, as its Director of Education. In his previous post as Education Director in Croydon he had implemented a framework of testing in schools which was to foreshadow that of the National Curriculum. His thinking had an undoubted influence on the educational policies of the Tory administration of the 1980s. Donald Naismith's brief was to make Wandsworth schools popular with parents, to raise the standard of examination results and to solve the major problem of more than 3,000 surplus places.

The Director of Education felt that specialist schools and courses could benefit Wandsworth schools. Once again his thinking was to influence later national policy. A party of six heads and officers were taken to the USA in February 1990 on a fact-finding tour of specialist or magnet schools.

The heads, however, were unable to give wholehearted support to the authority's enthusiasm for magnet/specialist schools:

> We were not able to examine magnet schools/programmes within the context of the whole of the American education service and thus we cannot form judgements about the effectiveness of magnet specialist provision in improving students' performance and attainment in the primary or the 11–16 secondary school sector.

Indeed, we have doubts about the wisdom of students specialising too early in their education. Specialist provision in the 16+ phase of education is a different matter. A ration of magnet programmes in this phase may be worth considering as one way of increasing collaboration between schools, colleges and Adult Education Institutes. Despite the favourable input of resources in the magnet schools/programmes that we saw, the pedagogy in the 3–19+ age range was not impressive. In our view, it was less effective than is generally found in schools in the UK. Our basis for forming this view rests on members of the group's experience in working for a significant number of LEAs besides the ILEA. In the UK the roles and responsibilities of teachers are greater and more onerous than in the USA. For example, our teachers carry out pastoral and disciplinary roles. In the USA classroom teachers are supported in their work by Deans of Discipline, Security Guards and Guidance Counsellors. We found that the level of administrative and clerical staffing in US schools was greater than in our own. The National Curriculum will move education away from too early specialisation, whether vocational or academic. There is a tension between the specialisation of magnets and the subject/content requirements of the National Curriculum, as in the USA there is only a very limited core curriculum. We consider that magnets carry with them considerable dangers of too early specialisation based on superficial information and rather random choice procedures which, in the long term, deny equality of opportunity.

The Future of Education in Wandsworth (1990)

The heads' views pre-dated those of a DES report published later in the year, *Teaching and Learning in New York City Schools*. This report showed little enthusiasm for specialist programmes in New York.

They are not offered across the city and the variable levels of support and funding they create tend to increase the gap between the best and the worst. They do not affect most schools and pupils. The 'pecking order' of schools is by and large retained and few schools can aspire to the excellence of some: in the words of one of our American speakers 'the best is not known to the most'.

(DES, 1990b)

The governing bodies of all Wandsworth secondary schools rejected the plans for specialist schools, as did the Parents' Consultative Committee and the headteachers. The authority initially denied that magnets would lead to a percentage of the intake being selected, but it soon became apparent that this was the case. There was the familiar parallel between Wandsworth and national policy. Wandsworth's 1992 document *Diversity and Choice* appeared a few months before the government's *Choice and Diversity* and covered some of the strands of the latter paper. In spite of the views of Wandsworth secondary heads, specialist schools were firmly on the political agenda.

Burntwood continued to be popular with parents. The governors had requested that the Education Committee increase, once again, the standard admission number from 210 to 240 a year. In spite of this increase, the standard admission number remained oversubscribed.

The 'magnet' or 'specialization' scheme appeared to threaten the autonomy of a girls' school. Why should a successful school implement a programme of magnet courses? Wandsworth's first magnet scheme envisaged movement of pupils between schools at the age of 14 but then moved to one by which pupils were chosen on their aptitude for a certain subject at the age of 10+. To the governing body this appeared to be a more spurious and inaccurate form of selection than the old 11+ examination based on general ability. Several of our governors had seen a televised interview given by the head of a City Technology College (CTC) in which applicants were asked 'And what musical instrument do you play at home?' They feared such selection which they saw as social. Wandsworth had given public encouragement to the setting up of a CTC within its boundaries and was to pioneer the first LEA CTC. Both were founded on selection through interview as well as testing.

Burntwood's governors saw magnets as a threat to its entity as a girls' school. The authority and not the school would ratify the specialism. This posed the potential problem of other schools being given science, maths or technology specialisms and Burntwood being given a 'soft' subject 'appropriate' in the eyes of the Education Committee to the education of girls.

The prospectus states that 'the school has a seriousness of purpose and aims for academic success but also to develop caring civilized students who will be the "women of tomorrow". We believe strongly in single-sex education for girls as it gives them that calm space of time in which to establish the foundation stones of later achievements.'

Specialist courses at a particular school could work and indeed the ILEA had operated one for music at Pimlico School but in the form of a borough-wide imposition they could quickly produce a pecking order of schools as indeed existed among New York schools. Burntwood had welcomed Wandsworth's open publishing of schools' examination results. We were not afraid of competition but this scheme could change our intake as well as that of other schools.

The governors believed that Burntwood should offer a broad and balanced curriculum. The Burntwood curriculum is an extended one offering pupils Latin, two modern languages, Dance and Drama.

Attempts at compromise with the authority were made by governing bodies and heads – offers to become a technology borough, for example, or to set up a system of schools as centres of excellence for different subjects on an afternoon a week. Both met with rejection. The Education Committee was not willing to follow the advice contained in the Association of County Councils Audit Commission's occasional paper of 1989 entitled *Losing an Empire, Gaining a Role*. The paper referred to the necessity of power-sharing:

> Nominally, schools and colleges are an integral part of the local education author-
> ity. In the past that has been very largely the fact as well as the formal position.
> Most expenditure and resourcing decisions have been taken by the LEA, that is
> by the elected members of the authority within a framework of national laws and
> regulations and with the advice of officers.
>
> Even before the Education Reform Act a trend towards greater delegation was
> beginning to become apparent, though on nothing like the scale now envisaged.
> In future, the LEA will still determine the aggregate budget, but many more

expenditure and resource decisions will instead be taken by governors of schools and colleges. In particular, staffing levels and appointments at individual institutions will be their own responsibility. This major change will remove the LEA's detailed control over those institutions.

The extent to which schools are prepared to enter into a partnership with the LEA will depend on the extent to which they share its educational philosophy. Where they do not, they may look for a more distant relationship or, indeed, seek to opt for grant maintained status. One authority has chosen to describe the nature of the relationship it seeks to establish with its institutions as that of a 'club'. The analogy is a good one. Schools will not participate in planning and collaborative activities unless they accept the club's rules and share its objectives.

Education committees will need to think more about the future. They must understand clearly that their direct management role has gone. They will need to plan more carefully, and to devote more effort to reviewing performance, if they are to fill the quality control functions envisaged for them under the Act.

Wandsworth Education Committee had no intention of losing its managerial role. Capital funding would be directed to schools developing specialisms. Most of the borough's secondary schools had been built as part of the ILEA's movement to comprehensive schools in the 1960s. They had been well designed by GLC architects, but were now at the stage of needing a radical overhaul. Burntwood's science laboratories were poor, indeed some were merely classrooms, and its craft, design and technology (CDT) facilities were inadequate. A survey by Wandsworth architects indicated that for purposes of sound maintenance alone the school needed £5 million spent on it as quickly as possible. The flat roofs were full of leaks, the heating system constantly failing, and the windows, because of rotting frames, in high winds blew into the classrooms to such an extent that pupils had to be sent home early for their own safety.

Burntwood governors unanimously decided to take advantage of the 1988 Education Act to seek GM status. There was a certain irony in an ex-ILEA governing body deciding to take this route. This difficult decision was taken for reasons of philosophy, but also as an answer to resolve the problem of capital monies. In 1991/92 four of Wandsworth's secondary schools opted out, leaving only three schools as specialist schools. It remains to be seen whether the new selective/specialist persona of these schools will transform them in the eyes of parents.

The Secondary Heads Association (SHA) recommends heads to play the role of an 'honest broker' in debates about GM status for their schools. I could not play the neutral role envisaged by SHA, but wished to associate myself fully with the views of the governing body. The case for GM was clearly presented to parents at a public meeting with speakers for and against and we received appoximately 80 per cent of the parent vote in favour of moving to GM status. The authority did not oppose, but in line with its principles, supported our move to GM. Burntwood's teaching and support staff voted by 60 per cent to back GM.

The transitional phase of moving to GM involves a substantial workload and this was carried by the Chair of Governors, the Head and the Deputy Heads. Burntwood was fortunate in that the Chair of Governors, Dr Judith Scott, was of exceptional ability and prepared to give generously of her own time whilst carrying a substantial workload for the Open University. It is hard to envisage the load of work facing the Chair of Governors during the months of transitional status (the period after the parents' vote but before DFE approval) and transfer to GM being combined with a full-time job. Are we moving to a time when with more autonomous self-governing schools we need a salary paid to the chairs of school governors similarly to those currently paid to the chairs of hospital trusts?

The Chair of Governors and the Vice-Chairs drew up a completely new *modus vivendi* for the governing body. It was made clear to the members of the new governing body that they would be expected to play an active role, not only in visiting the school, but in the statutory and standing committees which were to meet monthly. The committees, and particularly their chairs, have significant responsibilities – for example, in health and safety, pay policy, staff discipline and grievance, previously the ultimate responsibility of the LEA. There has been a major shift in the closeness of the governing body to the school. It was significant that governors of both the major political parties, appointed with party hats, chose to drop these when nominated for the trust governors, instead using other categories of their expertise, e.g. higher education, business, community or youth council, as they saw these as more appropriate. This was in stark contrast to the manner in which some governing bodies in London schools had been fraught with party-political arguments.

The Chair of Governors drew up a comprehensive structures and procedures document (July 1991). She outlined the extent of governors' responsibilities:

> Governors have to have policies on and exercise effective responsibility for:
> - *the curriculum* (including arrangements for inspections, complaints, school sessions and times)
> - *annual development plan* (review of current and discussion of new)
> - *staffing* (appointments and dismissals, pay and conditions, induction and training, discipline, grievances and appeals, trade union recognition, appraisal)
> - *finance* (budgets, audits, changing policies, insurance, fund-raising)
> - *buildings and grounds* (capital investment, maintenance, energy conservation, lettings and caretaking)
> - *admissions* (capacity, criteria, arrangements, appeals)
> - *health and safety*
> - *equal opportunities*
> - *school meals* (statutory duty to provide for pupils)
> - *governor training*
> - *Annual Report and parents' meeting*
> - *school prospectus*
> - *whole-school policies*
> - *community links* (with parents, other schools/colleges, ethnic communities, local industry)
> - *policies yet to be decided*

Structures

There are various ways in which the Governing Body can discharge its responsibilities:
- *full Governing Body*
- *sub-committees* with or without delegated powers. (A sub-committee *with* delegated powers would have the power to make decisions which would be reported back to the full Governing Body and minuted with no power of veto by the other governors)
- *ad hoc committees* for 'one-off' purposes, with or without delegated powers
- *individuals* (especially Head, Deputies and officers of the school)
- *links with school structures*, e.g. task forces, cross-curricular and departmental teams
- *visits* (how to make these effective)

Procedures

We need to:
(a)   decide which structures are most appropriate for the exercise of each responsibility;
(b)   establish terms of reference and membership of each structure, bearing in mind that we shall have to allow for new governors to be incorporated. Note that all committees can co-opt non-governors but that these members have no voting rights;
(c)   establish an annual timetable such that the full Governing Body and its sub-structures operate smoothly with each other to cover all responsibilities at appropriate times of the term/year; certain fixed items need to be incorporated into the timetable:
    - Annual Development Plan
    - budget and audit
    - Head's reports
    - prospectus
    - exam results
    - presentations on the curriculum
    - Annual Report to parents
    - election of Chair and Vice-Chairs;
(d)   decide on the employment of a competent Clerk to the Governors.

Communications

As the body solely responsible to the parents for the school and as employers of the staff, we shall have to consider ways of communicating and consulting with parents and staff.

Suggested Division of Functions

Full Governing Body

- curriculum (plus inspections, school sessions and times, complaints)
- Annual Development Plan
- discipline (rules and attendance)
- admissions policy (capacity, criteria, arrangements)
- equal opportunities
- governor training
- whole-school policies
- staff appraisal

Standing Sub-committees

1. Staffing
    – appointments and dismissals
    – pay and conditions
    – discipline (including exclusion and dismissal)
    – grievances
    – TU recognition
2. Finance
    – budgets
    – audits
    – charging policies
    – insurance
    – fund-raising
3. Buildings
    – capital investment
    – maintenance
    – energy conservation
    – lettings
    – caretaking
4. Exclusions
    This sub-committee must consist of at least three governors (excluding the Head and any governors on the Exclusions Appeal Committee) who decide whether or not to uphold the Head's proposals for exclusion.
5. Health and safety
6. School meals
7. Community links

Appeal Committees

1. Staff dismissals
2. Exclusions
3. Admissions.

In spite of the Chair of Governor's clarity, the governing body still suffers from the lack of involvement on the part of some governors. We have a few 'ghosts' at the full meetings and some do not fulfil the requirement that all governors should serve on a sub-committee. The load of the work, after the Chair, falls on those members who are willing to carry it.

The first year of GM status was similar to the first year of the amalgamation, in that the governors and senior team had the sense of once again setting up a new school. We did not, as in 1986, have to involve staff in the creation of an ethos, but new ways of working had to be established and the structures of the school once again reviewed. These internal changes flowing from GM have taken place in the framework of another externally imposed change, that of the National Curriculum. Implementation of this has been a huge management-of-change exercise for schools. It involved changes in the length and framework of the school day, and changes in the deployment and specialisms of teachers, with radical implications for resourcing.

A major difference between the concerns of the governing body in 1986 and 1992 was that finance has become the obvious and necessary key to the successful management of all schools, in the context of the LMS legislation. Governors at the time of the amalgamation had no responsibility for finance. GM status is, from the perspective of finance, an extension of LMS, and the Annual Maintenance Grant is tied to the LEA's LMS scheme until 1994. Only four years ago it was possible to be a head with a minimum interest in budgets; this is no longer the case – all decisions in schools have financial implications. We did not have sufficient expertise on the governing body, in the school office or amongst the senior team to be confident that we could handle the major areas of finance, personnel and administration that we were taking over from the LEA. We decided, as a deputy head was retiring, to use this post to finance the appointment of a Director of Finance and Administration.

We were not seeking some solitary expert issuing wise advice from his office divorced from the reality of the school – the education of pupils. We wanted someone who would play a full part in all senior team and middle management meetings, informing us not only of the financial perspectives of proposed decisions, but having an opinion equal in weight to that of any other member of the team. Our candidate was appointed by advertisement in the financial page of the *Guardian* and his post has the status of a deputy head. He is not concerned with pupil discipline, but has taken part in the senior team's programme of classroom observation and attends all major school functions. He is, in his role as Clerk to the governing body, essential to the smooth communication of all decision-making. I feel certain that eventually LMS/GM status will throw up a new breed of teacher candidates with MBAs and major school management responsibilities under their belts – but although a few such have been appointed they are as yet thin on the ground. The GM status of the school, with the advice of the Director of Finance, has led to the development of a 'value for money' culture which was not there before. The senior team has learnt that any divide between curriculum and finance is artificial.

A school becoming GM immediately presents a holistic face to the senior team and governors – there is no LEA responsible for particular groups of staff. A review of all areas of support staff was carried out by the governors. The autonomous school quickly gets rid of the culture of two staffs – support and teaching. All staff know that their future is bound up with the success and reputation of the school. All must play a part in presenting a 'good' school to the pupils and parents whether this be a school kept clean by the site teams, a school with documentation well produced by the media resources area, popular canteen facilities manned by the school's caterers, or sound classroom teaching by the professionals.

The senior team made the decision to change the titles of the Headteacher and Deputy Headteachers to those of Principal and Deputy Principals to acknowledge the changes brought about by GM to our roles and functions which now embraced responsibility for every member of teaching and support staff working in the building. The governing body has recognized unions/associations and has been careful to consult them in the preparation of its grievance, disciplinary and pay policies. This area of personnel needs much careful work; the governors of GM schools have major responsibilities as employers and Burntwood's have been careful to seek outside advice when necessary.

The authority had begun to reorganize its schoolkeeping services which were costly and inefficient. The governors and the senior team now had their own opportunity to reform this area. They did not choose to go down the LEA path of major cuts in personnel but instead to emphasize the 'better value for money' principle. A Site Manager's job was advertised with a far-reaching job description; the post was won against outside competition by Burntwood's Schoolkeeper.

The Site Manager's job description brought the postholder firmly into the middle management structures of the school. There were three main areas of responsibility: those of the day-to-day running of the site, responsibility as a budget head for allocation and monitoring of all monies within this heading, and the setting up of a Buildings Development Programme. The Site Manager acts as consultant to the governing body's Site Sub-committee. New structures of two teams of three, working in shifts, were devised. Site staff were required to become multi-skilled and to carry out minor repairs; no longer were there lengthy breaks in the mess room!

One of the benefits of GM status has been in dealing with the DFE rather than the LEA over financial matters. The Annual Maintenance Grant tie-in with the local LMS scheme has been complicated and had led to considerable delays. In contrast, the system of making bids for capital and special purpose grants to the DFE has been a smooth process of communication, with our queries clearly and quickly answered by the Department. Bids such as those for in-service training and minor/major works (formula allocation) have led us to examine and justify our priorities in a way we did not do before GM status.

Burntwood was extremely fortunate in gaining a capital grant of £500,000 as part of the government's technology initiative. In common with many girls' schools, we had inadequate technology facilities. This was now able to be rectified. As part of this successful bid we were able to initiate technology in languages by computer networks and 'state of the art' sound systems. We were also successful in our bid to be part of Toyota's Science and Technology Fund. One of Toyota's managers had initially looked at CTCs: 'but just how many CTCs would our fund support – one or two? We did not feel that we could get a national impact with that.' The company's research suggested that showpiece schools were not the best way of spreading good practice.

The second year of GM saw Burntwood make another successful capital bid for £800,000 for science facilities and the replacement of rotten window frames.

Major building works in parts of the school have affected classroom teaching, but teachers have shown considerable patience in the face of noise and other disruptions. Possibly our schools are so starved of capital monies that we as a profession are prepared to bear almost anything if the end result is a modern, well-resourced classroom. Pupils entering most state schools encounter a very different environment from the one they would meet in, for example, an airport, a shopping mall, a hotel or an office. Are we teaching our students that education is cheap, shoddy and outdated? Our buildings, like those of the majority of other state schools, were in a parlous state – we continually patched, mended and made do.

The first year of GM status was an exhilarating one. It revealed the LEA as an emperor without clothes – it was hard to remember the value of any of its services. The most liberating factor about GM status is how quickly minor changes, but changes that enhance the working conditions of both staff and students, can be effected. We have, for example, enhanced staff salaries, successfully bid for increased Section 11 funding, improved the standard of school cleaning and catering, improved working conditions for teachers in their departmental areas and increased the funding spent directly by the different subject areas.

Burntwood was fortunate to have been part of this new framework for schools. The autonomy of GM status has allowed us to develop as a better-managed institution and a more effective school. It has also given us the opportunity to develop unhampered by the constraints of an LEA whether of the political right or left. That control limited the effectiveness of the school.

GM status did not, however, give us the complete autonomy from the LEA which the governing body had envisaged. The Education Committee continued its programme of specialist schools, even tempting a comprehensive Church of England school from a neighbouring LEA to transfer to Wandsworth to become a specialist music school. In 1993 the LEA moved away from the selection criteria of 'specialist' to that of 'general ability' for the selection of pupils for its boys' school. Equal opportunities legislation meant, ironically, that the 90 places offered had to be matched with selected places for girls. The LEA asked Burntwood's governors to consider the issue of parity of provision, which if not matched by the school would be resolved by the creation of a new girls' grammar school in the borough.

The irony in this situation was that Burntwood already had, with its annual entry of 283 pupils, about 90 a year who met the Wandsworth selection criteria. Reluctantly the governing body took the pragmatic decision to accept selection of 30 per cent of the entry as the only way to safeguard our mixed intake as a comprehensive school. The transition to GM status had provided autonomy but the policies of the LEA had led to a context of selection which we could not ignore. We had been drawn into this context by equal opportunities legislation, but another mixed GM school had already opted for the selection of 50 per cent of its intake, which presented us with stiff competition. The complexities of choice and diversity remained.

CHAPTER 9

Tewkesbury School: the road to GM status

PAUL COTTER

Tewkesbury School is a co-educational comprehensive school of some 1,250 pupils between the ages of 11 and 18 years serving an extensive rural community. It became a GM school in April 1992. Appointed as its headteacher in 1985, Paul Cotter describes salient considerations leading to the decision to opt out of the LEA and the procedures involved in the process of achieving GM status. He also provides details of subsequent advantages and immediate financial and educational benefits in the self-management of the school, including those available through continuing co-operative working relationships with colleagues in the Gloucestershire Association of Secondary Heads (GASH) and various opportunities to buy back specialist educational services offered by the LEA to GM schools.

The introduction of LMS in the mid-1990s was based on the premise that schools would rise to the challenge of having more responsibilities devolved to them. LEAs became less prescriptive, and schools were given greater budgetary freedom to take into account their own local circumstances, needs and priorities. This new-found freedom was to be exercised through 'virement', the facility for moving funds within the overall budget, allowing schools to benefit directly as a result of good housekeeping and the achievement of greater efficiency. Thus savings on energy, cleaning, maintenance of grounds and premises could be turned into extra teachers, smaller classes, support staff, textbooks or computers. In other words, the school's budget could be deployed more efficiently for the benefit of its students and the quality of their learning. Unnecessary waste would disappear and the benefits would be felt in terms of improved student success and greater parental satisfaction.

Such was the fairy tale that seemed to be coming true but with the LEAs as ugly sisters, it was to prove difficult for schools really to get the full benefit of going to the ball.

Problems with LMS in practice

In reality, schools had little opportunity to make the most of funds since LEAs retained a significant amount of the funding for central administration and a variety of other services, which were then available to schools free of charge. As time progressed, and the prospect of GM emerged, LEAs responded by retaining less at the centre and devolving more, in a futile attempt to persuade LEA schools that they were getting as 'level a playing-field' as GM schools. However, this was a myth, since LEAs can never devolve the last 5 per cent or so needed to pay the Chief Education Officer's salary, the rent, the electricity bills and all the other fixed costs at County Hall. This 5 per cent is worth £100,000 per annum to a school of Tewkesbury's size. The perception of Tewkesbury School was that with more responsibilities devolved, the need for the LEA was diminished, and the incentive to opt out greater.

The weakness of the LEA position was compounded by the fact that despite the move to give more power and responsibility to schools, it was hard to detect any commensurate shrinking of the LEA machine. Indeed, on the contrary, administrative costs seemed to expand at both school and county level. It soon became obvious that if schools were to have extensive extra responsibilities, they would want to have the benefit of more cash to manage them, and the freedom to channel any surplus savings from a reduction in overall administration costs into the classroom for the benefit of children.

There was the additional problem of not knowing the extent of the devolution. Heads, being the suspicious creatures that they are, perceived an 'LMS trap', which was evident whenever schools faced an unexpected problem which was either costly or difficult to resolve. Who should pay for the rotting garage doors, the unblocking of sewage pipes, problems with the heating system, the leaking flat roofs and rodents in the rafters? The message seemed to be – 'The money has been devolved to you for this purpose and is somewhere in your budget.' This scenario became commonplace in times of educational cuts and was a constant cause of frustration and annoyance, creating an atmosphere of distrust between heads and LEA. It seemed that the LEA was happy to assist in the eventuality of a hurricane or an earthquake, but little else.

Tewkesbury School suffered harshly as a result of the vagaries of the Gloucestershire LMS scheme, and the crudity of the formula for allocating funds for premises which is determined purely by student numbers, taking no account of actual or historical costs. Given our extensive buildings, grounds and grossly inefficient heating system, our premises allocation was substantially underfunded as the figures in Table 9.1 clearly show.

Table 9.1. Shortfall on premises budget per annum (1992 values)

Energy, water and maintenance of premises	£20,000
Cleaning and grounds maintenance	£15,000

When we were an LEA school this had to be subsidized from the budget for teachers' salaries and was equivalent to a loss of almost two teachers per annum. It became impossible in times of cuts to protect existing class sizes, to keep teacher contact time below 0.8, and to maintain existing levels of spending on classroom materials without going into deficit.

Although it is desirable for an LMS formula to be clear, simple and predictable, it also needs to be just. Whilst Gloucestershire's scheme made allowances for small schools and transitional arrangements for those with high staffing costs, no such facility existed for schools with unusually high premises costs per student.

In view of this underfunding of our premises budget and a failure to persuade the LEA to modify the formula, the governors and I, who had been intensely loyal to the LEA, decided to 'seek our fortune' on the road to GM status.

How would opting out help?

The amount of extra funding we could expect to receive as a GM school was substantial as Table 9.2 shows. The figures are based on the unlikely situation that the LEA would be able to devolve as much as 95 per cent to the school for general spending, and retain only 5 per cent for central administrative purposes.

As a GM school we would also enjoy for the first time, the luxury of special purpose grants, which would allow us to have a staff development programme appropriate to the needs of 90 teachers and support staff; enough money to fund national curriculum changes adequately and to refurbish those parts of the buildings which the LEA had never reached.

Table 9.2. Tewkesbury School's levels of funding as an LEA and as a GM school

	LEA school (1991–92)	GM school (1992–93)
General allowance		extra £100,000
Special grants		
curriculum development	£5,000	£22,000
staff development	£5,000	£22,000
minor capital grants	limited and unpredictable	£30,000

In the first year there was also the added bonus of the transitional grant of £60,000, which was channelled into updating computer hardware for administrative purposes, establishing a computer network, introducing a new system to administer the finances, and making physical improvements to the school's central office.

The financial advantages of GM status soon became abundantly clear. The extra funding was the key that opened the door to better educational provision

– smaller classes, more support staff, better training and more classroom materials. At last we were receiving what the LMS schemes had promised to provide but which had proved so elusive – the opportunity to direct more money into the classroom.

Ironically, the more-forward-looking LEAs such as Gloucestershire had, with their effective LMS training of heads and governors, inadvertently paved the way for the latter to take the next logical step from LMS to GM status!

How painful was the progression to GM status?

Although many of the transitional tasks were time-consuming and complicated, the opting-out process itself was relatively stress-free. The strategies adopted are well worth repeating for those schools about to 'take the plunge'.

The governors and I had a policy throughout of keeping the various parties informed and involved in the debate – teachers, support staff, trade unions, parents, older students within the school and the LEA. The local media assisted with the impartial dissemination of information and kept the debate and the issues in the public eye. I believe this had the added advantage of ensuring that over 50 per cent of parents voted, thus avoiding the necessity of a time-wasting second ballot. Governors and school staff came together on a number of occasions to seek further information and to air anxieties. The governors decided after the first resolution had been passed that the teachers and support staff should be allowed to express their views in a secret ballot on the question of 'Whether opting out was right for Tewkesbury School?' The governors agreed to be guided by the outcome of that vote when considering a second resolution to ballot parents. This democratic gesture was appreciated by the staff, so that when their ballot result showed a majority in favour of opting out, those who had voted against gave their support to the final decision.

Governors were sensitive to the fact that many staff were worried that their existing conditions of service might be changed for the worse once LEA protection was removed. An assurance was given by the governors to those employed within the school that their conditions would be maintained and that trade union rights would continue to be recognized.

Those who would have opposed any move to make the school selective in any way were similarly reassured by the governors that the admissions policy would remain the same, and that students would continue to be allowed equal access regardless of ability or domestic circumstances.

The whole procedure leading to the acquisition of GM status was inevitably a lengthy one, but minimized and accomplished in seven months as a result of forethought, careful planning and a co-operative and intelligent response from officials at the Department for Education (DFE) and the Electoral Reform Society.

The Transitional Co-ordinator (a deputy head) made sure that tasks were equitably allocated to appropriate parties, and that these were completed and put into operation at the earliest possible juncture. Table 9.3 shows this process in action. For instance, the 'Application' and 'Proposals' for the acquisition of GM status had been prepared before the results of the parental ballot were known – a calculated risk but one which in itself shortened the opting-out process by about a month.

Table 9.3. Programme for the transition to GM status

First week in September – FIRST RESOLUTION PASSED
Gathering of information, consultation with staff and parents, staff ballot. Compiling of electoral roll.

First week in October – SECOND RESOLUTION PASSED
Parents' public meeting, period for checking electoral roll, ballot papers distributed by Electoral Reform Society, preparation of 'Proposals' and 'Application', governors draw up policies required for submission to DFE.

Last week in November – BALLOT OF PARENTS COMPLETED

End of first week in December – 'PROPOSALS' and 'APPLICATION' POSTED, and PRESS STATEMENT ISSUED
Start of transitional arrangements such as negotiating insurance, payroll and other service agreements.

Last week in February – PERMISSION GRANTED BY DFE

1 April – INCORPORATION AS GM SCHOOL

The financial benefits of an early incorporation date are plain to see. Of the additional funds illustrated in Table 9.2, a school of our size starting in April would get the full amount in the first financial year as a GM school, whereas a September start would provide 7/12ths, and January start only 3/12ths, of the extra money.

The moral dilemma in deciding whether to opt out

From what I have described, it all sounded too good to be true. However, throughout the whole process, the concern for many of us was that if Tewkesbury School opted out other schools remaining in the LEA would be financially disadvantaged, inevitably harming the children who attended them. These concerns were strongly vocalized at the public meeting for parents prior to the ballot, when parents expressed a wish that our partner primary schools should not suffer as a result of our intended action. Throughout the period of the debate, however, the LEA made no attempt to quantify the loss to those schools, so no assessment could be made as to whether the local primaries would lose hundreds or thousands of pounds each year if we opted out. Nevertheless it is fair to conclude that as the number of LEA schools declines, the burden of paying for the fixed costs of running the administrative centre of the authority is increased for those remaining. A legitimate response to this criticism is to argue that all schools have the right to apply for GM status, thus avoiding any possible financial penalties resulting from the departure of others.

Nor must it be forgotten that there is an onus on the LEA in these changing circumstances to attempt to reduce the size of its central administration in direct proportion to the number of schools opting out. In the longer term most fixed costs become variable and reduction can be achieved. There is also undoubtedly scope for LEAs to improve their efficiency as the following two striking examples illustrate.

Before incorporation the legal boundaries of Tewkesbury School had to be agreed with the LEA. This was an uncomplicated business even though a primary school and special school shared our campus. No fewer than five officials turned up to represent the LEA for the meeting on site.

Further, when the Deputy Head went to County Hall on a separate occasion to negotiate terms for the LEA to provide our personnel services, she was greeted by five LEA officials who attended the meeting. Obviously five is a significant number in Gloucestershire, but a more sensible number might have been one or two.

Although I had mixed feelings about the justice of government policy which allowed one category of school within the state sector to be funded more advantageously than another, I had no doubt that opting out was in the best interests of the students of Tewkesbury School in the short term and in the longer period. I was also convinced that it was my duty as head to advise governors, and ultimately parents, to consider the option of becoming grant maintained.

As a GM school we did our part to preserve the economic viability of the authority and to alleviate the loss to remaining LEA schools, by buying the bulk of our services from Gloucestershire. The latter had served us well in most respects over the years, particularly in terms of curriculum and administrative support. The close link between the school and LEA officers and inspectors was too valuable to be sacrificed. Gloucestershire LEA, to its credit, responded to the GM threat positively, with a clear commitment to serve the children in the state sector as effectively as it could, by radically reviewing its role as a service provider and thus improving its efficiency. It made a determined effort to bid competitively to provide us with services, and we agreed to purchase the following on three-year contracts linked to the retail price index:

> Payroll
> Personnel
> Curriculum advice
> Helpline to education officer
> Admissions
> Auditing

In addition, associate membership of the LEA gives us preferential rates for the purchase of LEA in-service courses and publications. The only service we could not buy for legal reasons was insurance – this was to prove to be a merciful escape, given that the company providing insurance cover for the LEA subsequently experienced financial difficulties.

The dangers facing the opted-out school

Although LMS was initiated to encourage proper expenditure on the things that really mattered in schools, it also encouraged heads to become preoccupied with budgets and the perennial question – 'Who pays?' Many heads can talk with more confidence about the contents of their balance sheets than about what goes on in their classrooms. They can explain the technicalities of LMS more easily than they can describe what is being done to help any underperforming teachers or departments within their own schools. Formal meetings of heads rarely contain an agenda item remotely connected to how to improve the delivery of the curriculum, the professional development of teachers and support staff, how to enrich the educational experience of students, or measure student achievement more accurately than reliance on crude tables of examination results. A new breed of head has evolved who is first and foremost a managing director, who acts as unqualified accountant and part-time entrepreneur.

With this preoccupation with LMS matters, it is easy for heads to become paranoid (often with good reason!), convinced that the LEA is 'out to do them down' with the intricacies and apparent contradictions of the workings of LMS. Heads' opinions about the LEA tend to swing dramatically – one moment the officers are schemers, the next they appear to be uninformed. The truth probably lies somewhere in between. These feelings became exacerbated in Gloucestershire during three successive years of cuts, particularly since heads were never precisely informed of the true extent of the cuts, nor of the reasons for them. In view of the fact that the most likely reason for the severity of the cuts is that Gloucestershire has too many small, uneconomic secondary and primary schools, the reticence is easy to comprehend.

In times of budgetary constraint, it is inevitable for heads to become obsessed with resource input rather than educational output. Equally the newly liberated GM head is prone to become besotted with his new bureaucratic toys and financial systems, not to mention all those monthly returns to the DFE. Herein lies the first peril – the risk of losing sight of the main purpose of the school's existence, the education of children, in the face of all these tempting distractions.

One justifiable major preoccupation occurred when Tewkesbury School was in the process of opting out. Inevitably there was a lot of small print to read in the seemingly 'endless' DFE papers, the ballot to organize, the 'Proposal', 'Application' and policies to prepare, service contracts to arrange and a proliferation of meetings with governors. However, once 'incorporated', the deputies and I had very much less external administrative work than before, allowing us once again to take a more active interest in the curriculum and the quality of classroom performance. This change in emphasis has been the result of three factors at Tewkesbury School:

(1)   The employment of a talented and energetic Business Manager.

(2)   An increased dependence on the business and professional skills of the governors. The expertise of the new governing body was strengthened in this regard with the addition of a solicitor, a bank manager and an accountant, the last being ideally suited to become our Responsible Officer.

(3)   The removal of any need to satisfy the bureaucratic requirements of the LEA after we had become a self-managing school. It was difficult to avoid coming to the conclusion that the LEA, with its proliferation of departments and officials, had generated an abundance of unnecessary paper work and bureaucracy. The fact that the DFE required significantly less in comparison came as a surprise after all the scaremongering about the hazards of working with civil servants who were based in London. I have found DFE employees affable, highly efficient, accessible (a phone call away) and decisive.

There is a second danger which can stem from the first. There are great perils for the school which believes it can flourish in isolation and develop the curriculum without the benefit of the experienced, objective, critical external eye. The head with delusions of being a finance director of a multinational company may be reluctant to spend money in areas where the return is difficult to quantify and certainly not on educational advisers costing over £350 a day. However, improving the quality of teaching and learning is an ongoing developmental process, needing more frequent evaluation and outside input than the occasional HMI visit and four-year inspection cycles. In addition to employing advisers, use can also be made of the experience to be found in other schools on a reciprocal basis with minimal financial cost. For instance, the deputy head responsible for staff development at Tewkesbury School works with two neighbouring schools, one having GM status and the other being an LEA school, in monitoring the progress and development of each other's newly qualified teachers. Joint INSET sessions with staff from neighbouring schools also occur much more frequently. The school's Business Manager is in frequent contact with his opposite numbers in other GM schools, with the result that expertise and experience can be shared. There is no doubt that we can all learn from each other's successes and failures, and from the 'critical friend' who is not directly connected with our own institutions.

In addition, there are more formal structures which exist in Gloucestershire which ensure that schools communicate and discuss common issues. One mechanism is the Gloucestershire Association of Secondary Heads which makes no distinction between GM and LEA heads in terms of membership. This Association is a powerful body for negotiation and consultation with the LEA and other bodies. It has become an ideal vehicle for fighting proposed educational cuts, and for dealing with the media. There is another group comprising GM heads which regularly meets to exchange ideas.

A third danger for us was the loss of what had been an outstandingly successful area of activity: the partnership with our primary schools. In earlier years we had enjoyed a close relationship with our primary colleagues, which had been established through regular visits of pastoral staff, sessions to share and discuss classroom practice, teacher exchanges and pairings, and curriculum projects. It was vital that our GM status did not put this good work in jeopardy by driving a wedge between us.

We therefore strengthened the best of existing practice by embarking on some new initiatives with the primary schools. Together we identified cross-phase and cross-curricular needs, and this has led to further exciting developments in a range of curriculum areas and embraced children of all ages. A similarly significant achievement was the joint INSET Day to address the problem of curriculum continuity and progression through the Key Stages. Given our enlarged budget we were able to find the money to finance the bulk of these initiatives.

A final danger was the potential for alienating local people, should the governing body in its new role as landlord choose to 'flex its muscles' through increased charges to the local College of FE which provides adult education classes, or the borough which hires our sporting facilities for public use in non-lesson time. In view of the governors' commitment to the maximization of community use of the complex, agreements were amicably reached which maintained previous custom and practice. Tewkesbury School is a community school in all but name, a feature recognized by the assessors for the Schools Curriculum Award in 1990 and the Queen's Jubilee Award in 1992. These prestigious awards were won on the sound basis of a desire to serve and be accountable to both the broader local community and parents, and to be influenced by their wishes. We, in turn, have been able to utilize the rich local resources. Many of our courses, extra-curricular initiatives, student placements in the community, workshops and curriculum projects have been dependent on the goodwill and generosity of the people who live and work in the Tewkesbury area. Hundreds of hours are donated to the school each year in the form of consultation, advice, expertise and the arrangement for work experience in its many guises. An added bonus has been the gifts of materials and money, for example – two minibuses; help with the creation of a careers centre and technology suite; £25,000 to purchase computers; kit for sports teams; and technology equipment.

Review of the benefits after twelve months as a GM school

The benefits have greatly exceeded expectations and are fundamentally in two categories:

>   (1)   The extra funding in 1992–93 through the Annual Maintenance

Grant and the special purpose grants has enabled us to overcome an LEA cut of £50,000, and generate a surplus of £100,000, whilst achieving the following significant improvements:

- a reduction in class sizes in Year 7 and achievement of an average class size of 26 students in Years 7 to 9, which is below the county average
- an expansion of the Key Stage 4 and post-16 curriculum
- spending 20 per cent more on classroom materials and £4,000 on the Schools' Library Service
- substantially improving the opportunities for staff training and development
- using supply teachers after one day's teacher absence (the LEA norm is three)
- employing two extra support staff
- employing paid invigilators for external examinations
- extending the peripatetic music tuition by 10 per cent
- refurbishment of student toilets and the creation of a second drama room
- purchasing a computer network and extending the central office accommodation
- doubling of the spending on the refurbishment and replacement of furniture
- appointing a Business Manager to relieve teachers and the senior management team of many administrative duties.

The major capital grant of £259,000 to replace our defunct and costly heating system was the icing on the 'First Anniversary Cake' – a source of future savings of £15,000 per annum, which will arise from improved energy conservation and fewer maintenance bills.

(2) We have been given genuine responsibility for our destiny with vastly increased scope to determine our own priorities in the best interests of the students within the school. There has been a removal of the LEA bureaucracy and the often lengthy time-scales, which were a constant source of frustration. The DFE machine is much less intrusive and more user-friendly. A fundamental role reversal has taken place in the relationship between the school and Gloucestershire LEA, with the latter's role changing from master to servant. GM schools, on the other hand, are the new masters buying only those services which represent value for money, as measured by the way they positively impinge on the quality of the teaching and learning, and the physical environment.

The future for GM schools and LEAs

Whilst it is impossible to predict the future with any certainty, it seems likely for the foreseeable future, under a Conservative government, that whatever the precise funding arrangements, GM schools will continue to receive substantially better funding than those schools in the LEA. The size of the Annual Maintenance Grant will reflect the extra responsibilities intrinsic to GM schools. The special purpose grants may, of course, vary in amount, but the one which brings substantial funding for curriculum and staff development (SPG D) is directly related to the national Grants for Education Support and Training (GEST) cake and is therefore likely to remain. There are two reasons why LEA schools have generally received a small fraction compared with GM schools. First, the LEAs have tended to spend the bulk of the GEST allocation on behalf of the schools without, I suspect, seeking prior approval from heads and governors. Second, the government gives GM schools preferential GEST funding.

Another bonus is the present government's commitment to giving GM schools 25 per cent of the funds available nationally for major capital improvements, regardless of the number of GM schools. Although the rationale is difficult to follow, one does not need to be a mathematician to deduce the potential gains and losses to the respective sectors.

As to the future of LEAs which have a sizeable number of GM schools, there needs to be a radical change in the way they market their services. LEAs would do well to use Gloucestershire as a model, and copy the way in which it has become more efficient at the centre, and has sought to devolve the maximum possible finance to its schools. It has thus forced itself to become an efficient provider of services to institutions, regardless of their type or geographical location. I suspect in the longer term individual departments within the LEA are likely to become self-financing, operating under service-level agreements. I believe there is a place for an LEA or a similar locally based body which can play a key role in serving the educational needs of schools and helping in the development work which is so important in raising academic standards. After all, the LEA will still be legally responsible for the quality of education in those primary and secondary schools which do not opt out.

GM schools such as ours will wish to purchase tried and trusted local services, operated by people who have established a long-standing relationship with the school, with one marked difference from the 'old days' – we will be less prepared to accept second-best.

CODA

In the concluding chapter, the editor considers possibilities for organization within the education system by the end of the century. Given a largely prescribed organizational framework, it is argued that schools should reflect earned leader–follower relationships amongst headteachers and their colleagues. Headteachers as 'professional leaders' rather than business managers will be required if full personal and professional commitment of teachers as positive contributors in the education of pupils within an informed and learning society is to be secured. It will be essential for self-managing schools to develop increasingly as effective educational organizations and not merely be managed as business enterprises.

CHAPTER 10

Towards 2000 – organization and relationships

VIVIAN WILLIAMS

> Organisation is a means to an end rather than an end in itself. Sound
> structure is a prerequisite to organisational health; but it is not health
> itself. The test of a healthy business is not the beauty, clarity or perfection
> of its organisational structure. It is the performance of people.
>
> (Drucker, 1980, p. 602)

Organizational structure

If Drucker's widely respected view is correct, the importance of sound organizational structure for the reformed education system is essential to the future well-being of its functioning into the next century. However, it has to be noted that the recent reforms of the education system do not at the moment present a convincing prospect for either clients or providers. One of the indices of a successful system is the high degree of confidence possessed by those who are required to work towards the achievement of organizational objectives. The degree of regulatory prescription and the failure to involve directly the 'people' on whom the recently mandated educational policies-in-action depend for success, lead to some doubt about the co-operation, enthusiasm and commitment with which the reforms are being introduced and implemented.

Clearly, the transition to a system of self-managing schools such as those considered in this book is leading towards an organizational framework of schools in England and Wales which will be fundamentally different from the national system of schools in existence for at least the past thirty years. Should the current pace of systemic change be sustained, it is possible that by 2000 these differences will be greater than the transition from pre-1960s selective secondary schools to the comprehensive school framework. However, it is clear that the transition to organizationally autonomous self-managing schools is emerging without the sustained support provided by the experience, expertise, detailed planning and professional consideration of LEAs or the collective views of elected members – all considerable influences in the planned development of secondary comprehensive schools during the 1960s and 1970s. During that formative period, the requirement of LEAs to submit holistic, coherent plans for graduated change in the status, character and size of schools following widespread consultation with parents and to secure the co-operation of teachers provided a portfolio of government strategies for systemic reform.

In retrospect, perhaps the most significant of the requirements to introduce systemic change through government policy in 1965 was that:

> The government are aware that the complete elimination of selection and separat-
> ism in secondary education will take time to achieve. They do not seek to impose
> destructive or precipitate change on existing schools; they recognise that the
> evolution of separate schools into a comprehensive system requires careful plan-
> ning by local education authorities in consultation with all concerned.
>
> (DES Circular 10/65, paragraph 46)

The contrast between systemic reform in the 1960s and government policies and ministerial attitudes during the past decade is both remarkable and, for many in the education service, regrettable. Further, and unlike the reforms in the comprehensivization of secondary education, current organizational reforms are being applied across the whole of the education system. For example, virtually every primary, secondary and special school has become self-managing. In addition, almost everywhere the transition has been implemented over considerably shorter time-scales than occurred in the majority of LEAs during the 1960s and 1970s.

Problems of choice and diversity

In its White Paper *Choice and Diversity* (DFE, 1992) the government reiterated its quintet of policy 'great themes' since 1979 and which provided the basis for the Reform Act of 1988. Rhetorically, the themes are: quality, diversity, parental choice, school autonomy and accountability. As broad policy objectives all are both laudable and uncontentious. But a serious imperfection is that the government has failed to consult with any of the major stakeholders who are central to the achievement of these thematic objectives.

It is true to say that the LEAs as traditional guardians and stewards of the educational policy objectives; teachers who are at the heart of all these endeav-
ours and without whose commitment none can be attained; parents who are genetically involved in the educational process; and other community interests such as employers and further and higher education establishments; may have been *informed* of government policy intentions but have been excluded from the process of policy *formulation*. For more than a century, the local government framework has diffused legitimate political power amongst many different organizations and interests. It has been predicated on a clear value base that it is important to ensure a diffusion of power which involves many decision-
making processes responsive to local needs and wishes. Ranson and Thomas (1989) place considerable emphasis on the importance of education as a

public good because of its ubiquitous significance. Education is a public good because its collective characteristics cannot be a selective matter for individuals acting alone. The quality of educational provision means that it is a matter of public choice which is accountable to that public as a whole. In Ranson and Thomas's view, the role of LEAs is to support and facilitate public involvement not only as consumers, i.e. parents and employers but also as members of communities. Nevertheless, without the benefit of consultation with the major client and provider interests, advice or focused research evidence, the organization of the national system has been reshaped by government *fiat* based on little more than pragmatic political reformist zeal and informed, if that is not too exaggerated a term, via somewhat flawed remote-sensing mechanisms of closed-circuit political caucus opinion.

Confidence in the new organizational framework of education, and its value system – a critical factor in the formulation of educational policies – is further undermined when government strategy is explicitly based upon value assumptions which are contentious and susceptible to widely different interpretations:

> More diversity allows schools to respond more effectively to the needs of the local and national community. The greater their autonomy, the greater the responsiveness of schools. Parents know best the needs of their children – certainly better than educational theorists or administrators, better even than our mostly excellent teachers.
>
> (DFE, 1992, p. 3)

Assumptions of this kind reveal an impoverished understanding of educational development by policy-makers and a failure to recognize the multiple partnerships essential to enduring development and achievement in educational processes. Attitudes implicit in this kind of rhetoric lead to polarization and adversarial relationships and not to mutually supportive partnerships that all schools require and every pupil deserves.

In addition, policies of 'diversity', whether through LEA-maintained or centrally funded GM schools, may lead, indeed have led, to mutation of a value system ostensibly geared to a determination 'that every child should have the very best start in life' (DFE, 1992, p. iii). With considerable regret the writer has to mention that since the Education Act of 1988 some schools have been unable, and others reluctant, to make adequate provision for pupils with special needs; to tackle problems over the attendance of pupils with behavioural difficulties; to make adequate financial provision for improved teacher–pupil ratios; or to provide funding for music tuition, field excursions, inter-school team games or visits to museums, art galleries or theatres. The government's policy may lead to its claimed 'robust' framework for the organization of schools and the provision of a National Curriculum. However, through policies for institutional choice and diversity it is evident that perceptions of *particular* headteachers, parents and communities have led to self-interested priorities in self-managing schools reflected in monocular perspectives rather than through binocular views hitherto arising from the natural differences in scales of perceptions of educational needs between schools and LEAs.

Inevitably, such issues are embedded in concepts of autonomy, accountability and local democracy. As considered by David Church in an earlier chapter, the emasculation of LEAs has led to the weakening, or removal, of a sense of belonging to a wider community within a publicly provided education *service* rather than a system. Within the organizational reforms of the 1988 and the 1993 Education Acts, the possibility exists that during the next few years former perceptions of an education service, provided for all maintained schools and controlled through a series of checks and balances within publicly accountable, democratically elected and visible local government all-purpose authorities, will be replaced by a government-controlled hierarchical appointed system. Accountability will no longer exist as an explicit public requirement but only between the government department, its quango-style organizations and individual schools, mediated principally through the OFSTED inspection mechanism and annual financial controls.

In effect, a new phase has emerged of management by government *ex-cathedra* regulation rather than through widely shared and diffused responsibility. Whilst acknowledging that local government organizations, including those in some LEAs, were imperfect and required refashioning together with improved monitoring and demonstrable accountability, it has to be said that government action in withdrawing all the major duties and responsibilities from LEAs because a few were perceived as having failed fully to discharge their statutory responsibilities and ignoring the major educational achievements of many other LEAs, appears both unnecessarily draconian and mistaken – damaging to educational purpose, practitioner commitment and democratic principles.

It is difficult to avoid reaching a conclusion that some form of district or regional education body as a facilitating, monitoring 'voice' will be required to ensure that all schools and pupils have genuine access to improved educational opportunities for realistic achievement of the government's five-theme policy. Similarly, the creation of such bodies would provide a forum for expression of interests or concerns among the major stakeholders. But unless such bodies were reflective of elected constituencies they would be neither democratic nor publicly accountable. Although the school board system in the USA would not appear to be a 'model' for adoption because of its limited perspective, concepts underlying this system, which seek to provide for community involvement at local and district levels within a democratic electoral framework, *might* offer ways in which specific local concerns and developments could be accommodated.

Without the existence of bodies specifically elected to oversee educational provision, there appears to be no place for a publicly accountable forum within the government's reformist policies that would provide legitimate opportunities for collective thinking, coherent planning or constructive tension in educational provision amongst the disparate interests dependent on promoting improved quality and achievement in the education system. It should be particularly disturbing for parents, employers and teachers to contemplate an educational system in the late 1990s controlled and operated by centrally appointed submissive and publicly unaccountable bodies established through a proliferation of governmental power extension via quango organizations reflecting a significant denial of local or national democratic processes.

For some, an ominous pointer towards increased central control has occurred through the establishment of the Funding Agency for Schools (FAS) and formulae for educational associations under the 1993 Education Act. Inevitably, parental/community interests and responsibilities will be constrained and subordinated to curricular, evaluative and financial controls by these and other agencies. It is difficult at this stage to envisage how elected members of school governing bodies or local communities will be enabled to play an effective role in decision-making forums for educational provision as part of a public service responsibility required to be both accountable and responsive to perceived needs beyond those existing at individual school level. Nevertheless, it is important to recognize that there are not merely significant issues about espoused values at individual school level influenced by the immediate ordering of priorities for pupils but also wider issues of societal values in the interpretation of legal and regulatory prescriptions; effective curriculum development and practice; in-service training for all teachers; co-ordinated provision for disadvantaged pupils; resource distribution among schools; and administrative matters such as the management of the physical environment, property and personnel. To be successful and effective, democratic processes require underpinning of support provided by trusted expertise, respected experience and mutual confidence between schools, their governing bodies and those employed to undertake a variety of essential management functions.

The concern expressed here about the reduction in opportunities for the exercise of democracy is not intended to deplore positive innovative government policies in the reform of the education service. Rather, the concern outlined is for an education service that appears to have been redesigned solely to secure increased central control over educational policies and practice. A widespread concern already exists that centralized organizational control will be achieved through bureaucratized regulatory insensitivity and that important stakeholders – pupils, parents, teachers and employers – who are both 'clients' and 'providers', will be marginalized with little sense of direct participation in the process of education. Marginalization would appear to have become an established political strategy.

Problems for schools

A further acute concern exists amongst teachers in schools over the perceived denial of any sense of 'ownership' of policy processes requiring major practitioner change in efforts for, and commitment to, pupils. In the reorganization of the system, many teachers believe government strategies have overlooked or deliberately ignored that it is at school level where policy prescriptions, mandated objectives, fiscal expansion or restraint are implemented by:

> those ... directly employed in schools ... who have to interpret and deliver policy-in-action programmes intendedly of immediate benefit to pupils and students and, in the longer term, to the communities ... they serve. The cutting edge of policy reform is most keenly experienced by teachers, pupils and students at school and college level ...
>
> (Williams, 1992, p. viii)

To secure commitment to values underpinning any major reform process requires a degree of participation in policy formulation of those expected or required to implement policies-in-action. In effect, those who have to 'carry the can' should participate in its design. Very few LEA, teacher, parent or governing body associations appear to have been involved in the formulation of government policies throughout the 1980s or during the early 1990s – a matter of fundamental concern for all client and provider interests and undoubtedly a source of many of the serious misgivings and adversarial attitudes to current policy intentions and implementation. There is a clear and demoralizing belief that a government policy of disempowerment of stakeholders is part of a not-very-well-hidden political agenda.

Superficially, the government appears to recognize these concerns:

> The process of change is never easy for those involved. Parents are naturally concerned about the implications for their children. Teachers worry about what it means for their pupils, their school and the burdens on them as they pursue their vocation. Managers throughout the education service have to be mindful of what it all costs, as well as what the reforms have to achieve. The Government recognises these concerns. The transformation of education we have undertaken is designed to ensure that our education system becomes the best in Europe.
>
> (DFE, 1992, p. 2)

It is somewhat ironic that such explicit recognition of the difficulties of major change processes has not been matched by an elementary understanding of how best that 'transformation' might be achieved – certainly it lies beyond the reach of a government that adopts such an instructional stance. There is no evidence in government policies of any sense of recognition of, or invitation to participate in, a 'partnership'. It is a *tour de force* of explicit central government power. Everywhere, there is prescription and regulation: the National Curriculum; testing and assessment; local management of schools; performance appraisal; and accountability. There are many persuasive arguments for the introduction of all of these policies but it is the manner in which they have been formulated, prescribed and introduced that has triggered widespread opposition. Beyond the government and the DFE virtually every educational interest has been relegated to roles of functionaries and not as thoughtful, active contributors in the development of a more effective education system. Many of the stated 'official' reasons for government reform have been based on negative perceptions, especially in relation to national economic competitiveness. Since 1979, every Secretary of State for Education has voiced trenchant criticism of the education system. As outlined by Lawrence (1992), Carlisle, Joseph, Baker, MacGregor, Clarke and, especially, Patten have been serially and explicitly negative about the operation and outcomes of almost every educational endeavour. Since 1979, the politics of educational denigration has flourished.

The determination of the government to take control of the education system, ostensibly for its contribution to economic growth, has supplanted earlier values about the importance of educational opportunities for the development of the individual which were core values in the 1944 Education Act. It has been argued that changing values and priorities are entirely justified and are appropriate contemporary objectives. If so, one has to ask if the ways in which reform has been introduced should have been expressed unequivocally in materialistic and economic rhetoric and not presented as an extension of 'grass-roots democracy', extended educational opportunity, increased local freedom and individual autonomy.

For example, the notion of 'parental power' politically trumpeted since the early 1980s is difficult to sustain. There is as yet little published evidence indicating that parents play a significant role in determining school priorities, content or focus of the curriculum, or teaching or learning styles. A recent study of the ways in which parents exercised choice over enrolment at schools for their children unsurprisingly indicates that these decisions aroused deep emotions intermingled with intellectual judgement in a 'tangled interplay of personal and general concerns'. The conclusions were that a balance was required between the right of parents to exercise relatively short-term individual preferences, possibly shifting and unpredictable, and the maintenance of a stable base for a long-term educational strategy (Morgan *et al.*, 1993). Similarly, a survey of the first 100 GM schools indicated that although it had been envisaged that parents would play an important role in decisions leading to the establishment of GM schools, only 4 per cent of the respondents in the survey named parents, other than those who were members of governing bodies, as advocates of opting out (Coleman *et al.*, 1993).

However, and although there appears to be no firm evidence, it is conceivable that greater involvement of parental decision-making will occur as more information about schools is published. For example, and in addition to the formal annual reporting to parents by the governing bodies of schools, publication of external examination results and school attendance rates, four-yearly OFSTED reports on individual schools and simplification of procedures to opt out, especially for 'grouped' primary schools, may lead to more active participation among parents. But at this stage, it is difficult to envisage (other than for issues in connection with designated school status or closures) parents playing directly significant roles in shaping the ways in which schools organize and provide opportunities for pupils. During the next few years it is likely that much more significant will be the development in roles played by the School

Curriculum and Assessment Authority (SCAA), the FAS and, where appropriate, school associations – all established and controlled by the Secretary of State and the DFE through the exercise of statutory powers.

It is evident that disquiet exists over the appropriateness of the structure of the reformed education system for the future educational development of schools. In applying the Drucker 'test', it is by no means clear that the organizational framework of the emerging system is as sound as it should be or that it will facilitate and encourage improved performance by those who are charged with implementing unilaterally determined policies. However, optimism for the future lies within the context of self-managing schools and the constrained freedom of LMS which provides opportunities for schools to choose ways in which the teaching and learning environment should be organized and resourced. Through those limited, but significant, freedoms, opportunities exist to release the many talents and skills and the commitment of teachers to develop schools as learning communities for pupils and adults. If more effective schools are to emerge during the next few years, it will be important to promote greater professionalization of teachers rather than to place trust in vacuous political rhetoric about reformist policies.

School organization

During the past two decades it has become fashionable to consider the 'culture' of schools as an 'envelope' term to subsume ethos, tradition, patterns of organizational behaviour and so on. In a seminal study of comprehensive education, Hargreaves (1982) examined issues associated with school cultures of *individualism* held as inimical to collectiveness, institutional loyalty and interdependence. In Hargreaves' view, these are evident in the disappearance of collective school rituals such as whole-school assemblies, school uniform and the replacement of the 'form' as an organizational pupil unit (both for enrolment and as a physical base) with varied pastoral care arrangements leading to an image of schools 'providing the Paddington Station effect every forty minutes' as pupils proceed to other rooms and teachers for serial time-tabled teaching periods. In other schools the Paddington Station scenario is replaced by 'the Luton Airport effect . . . as children stream round the buildings, but are now armed with huge cases, bags, carriers, hold-alls in which all their belongings are kept. There is no corporate home, no collective responsibility and yet teachers are puzzled that there is low institutional pride' (p. 89).

Whatever the arguments over such perceptions, they provide views of the organizational culture of schools. Smith and Peterson (1988) provide a useful definition of institutional culture in that it may be defined as 'agreed ways of interpreting signs, symbols, artefacts and actions'. The key word is 'agreed'. In schools, pupils, headteachers and their colleagues differ over ways in which organizational behaviour is perceived and interpreted. Thus, the culture of schools reflects those characteristics about which there is a general consensus amongst headteachers, teachers and pupils. Those who lie beyond the consensus establish their own sub-cultures – often at odds with the generally perceived and accepted norms of valuing the life and work of schools.

For Hargreaves, the development of a culture of individualism is not an opportunity to become nostalgic for the past and he also does not suggest that it has been a grievous error. His contention is that any educational system based on extreme cultural perceptions whether of *individualism* or *collectivism* must be fundamentally defective. His position is admirably clear: any system that is determined entirely by instrumental criteria such as prescribed social functions will lead to the sacrifice of individual considerations. Similarly, a system exclusively geared to individualism excludes recognition of social functions and its consequences which cannot simply be ignored or remitted to other mechanisms such as the hidden social agenda in schools.

The future well-being of schools will rest on clear understandings of how schools function and become more effectively organized during the next few years. It will be important to recognize the different contexts provided through the requirements of the Education Acts of 1988 and 1993. Although subject to the vagaries of political chance, it is difficult to avoid coming to the conclusion that a tiered education system will exist by 2000. Local authority maintained schools co-existing with directly funded grant-maintained schools in an open-enrolment 'pupil-market' competitive environment will lead to responsively selective, technological and magnet schools differentiated from 'other' schools in many localities. The effect will be to create a tiered élite of schools geared to market and self-interest considerations. The pressures on governing bodies, headteachers and their colleagues to become competitively thrusting, entrepreneurial managers of school enterprises will be considerable. Such narrow locally determined priorities may lead to reinforcement of an educational system focused on individualism rather than collectivism during the next few years. If so, it will have been predicated on fashionable ideological assumptions about the education 'market' as a more attractive and appropriate mechanism for controlling provision than earlier-established processes for educational planning graduated development at national and local levels as occurred in the 1960s.

Headteachers and systemic change

As is demonstrable from the contributions to this book, the positional status of the headteacher in responding to organizational changes introduced by LMS is the *pivotal* one. As schools must now operate in more sharply defined and politicized contexts at community and central government levels, headteachers are required to function within these new realities. To be successful, they and their colleagues in schools must be adequately prepared and become skilled in handling new situations with which increasingly they are confronted (Williams, 1989).

Since 1988, it is questionable whether any other publicly funded sector has been so inadequately prepared for fundamental changes in organizational responsibility. It is difficult to condone policies that remitted to governing bodies and headteachers direct responsibilities for annual recurrent budgets, typically in excess of £1.5 million in secondary schools, with scant preparatory training in the management of personnel, budgets and sites. That the majority of schools have accepted these obligations, coped with and, indeed, flourished under their new responsibilities should be a matter for public admiration and considerable gratitude. That these unprecedented changes have been successfully incorporated into school organization with concurrent sweeping reforms in the implementation of the National Curriculum and its associated assessment regime is even more remarkable. However, meeting these demands may have been achieved at considerable and, as yet, unanticipated costs. For example, a major concern is that in the future management of schools it will be difficult for headteachers to sustain their internationally admired traditional role of being first and foremost the 'leading professional' or as *primus inter pares* for their colleagues. Interestingly and significantly, during the past decade in North America, research studies on the development of 'effective schools' have centred on educational limitations of the role of school principals as *administrators*. Pressures have increased for recognition of the roles of school principals as instructional leaders – with emphases on their curricular and educational expertise. Former requirements of expertise in administrative and site-management skills are being reduced, in order to enhance their roles as educational leaders if schools are to develop as effective learning institutions. The trend is evident in recent 'preparation for principalship' courses as well as in post-experience higher degree studies leading to the required certification of principals in North America. Similarly, many in-service courses have explicit foci on curriculum development and learning theory, while former preoccupations with training in school law and financial management are losing ground.

Thus it appears somewhat odd that in England and Wales current trends and priorities appear to be developing in ways that are waning elsewhere. In our system, headteachers whose careers have been founded on demonstrable skills and experience as educators are now required to become familiar with and develop management expertise in accountancy, personnel and public relations and become well versed in the associated legal aspects of these functions. In preceding chapters, Brigid Beattie and Paul Cotter refer to personal perceptions in the changing role of the headteacher through moving towards managerial roles with similarities to those of business directors or chief executives. Other headteachers have parallel experiences and if the trend were to become established, governing bodies might seek to appoint headteachers more skilled in demonstrating expertise in financial and personnel management than in educational development. Thus, 'education' cultures of schools would be replaced by school business management environments – precisely the trend that many schools in North America now regard as obsolescent in the development of educationally 'effective schools'.

Leadership in schools: new directions?

Following the 1988 Education Act and recognition that its implementation would fundamentally alter relationships between clients and providers of education in the governance of schools, it was evident that new partnerships would lead to significant changes in roles among the stakeholders in the education service. At that time the foreshadowed realities suggested ways in which effective new relationships might emerge across conventional institutional, social and political boundaries to engage, inform and develop effective links with opinion leaders and stakeholders (Sayer and Williams, 1989).

Experience since then has indicated the extent to which the realities of these new relationships have emerged. With the exception of a few notable and highly publicized instances, schools have established and sustained admirable levels of co-operation and support within their communities. New procedures and styles in the governance of schools and for effective internal self-management have emerged. In contemplating further development of the partnerships during the next few years the imperative of *distributed leadership* in schools is perhaps the most pressing priority.

It is unnecessary here to examine in detail the view that organizations, including schools, consist of people who work within interdependent controlled arrangements to achieve collective objectives. However, it is important to remember that it is *people* who have objectives and the organization is only the mechanism necessarily established to ensure that objectives beyond the reach of an individual can be achieved through collective effort. To secure effectiveness and efficiency in attaining declared objectives, it is people who establish norms of behaviour and performance for achievement through controlling arrangements under which rewards and resources are allocated, or denied, to individuals and groups. Consequently, rules, regulations, procedures and conventions are used to facilitate and control behaviours of organizational members. These organizational requirements create the context and culture in which specialist roles and other functions are defined and partitioned with appropriate relative positional status and responsibilities identified. It is individuals and groups who are invested with authority to ensure that objectives are achieved through the co-ordination of collective effort. Organizational environments may be viewed as theatres where public and private roles are played on a broad stage. The dramas are about political and positional power for the control of people and other resources, ostensibly in the pursuit of effectiveness and efficiency but also, and not infrequently, for personal gratification – invariably at the expense of shared values, organizational purpose and collective interdependence.

Nevertheless, opportunities for a heightened sense of collectiveness and interdependence exist through the ways in which the educational system has been refashioned since the mid-1980s. Measures of reform take time for their effects to become apparent and comprehensible. Inevitably, they also lead to unexpected and unintended consequences. What is already evident is that teachers are required to develop new skills to secure effective collaboration involved in working together on a regular basis, in the taking of collective decisions and through team implementation of policies adopted. For most teachers working in teams has, or will, become a permanent and continuous reality. Those who work in schools are conscious that it is no longer the talented individual who is the sole architect of successful endeavour. Jay (1981, p. viii) puts it rather well: 'it is not the individual but the team which is the instrument of sustained and enduring success in management'. Although it has been known for many years that the effectiveness of groups is greater than the sum of its individual talents the truism has now assumed considerable significance in developing new cultures of organizational behaviour in schools.

In response to required government education policy change schools have developed formal organizational arrangements increasingly dependent on the existence of temporary or permanent 'teams', 'task groups' and 'working parties' in the search for school effectiveness and improved functioning. It is an inevitable trend as, for example, LMS policies are extended into the governance of schools with semi-autonomous departmental or faculty groups identified as cost-centres within overall school budgetary control. Given the legislated *fiat* for self-managing, local financial autonomy and client-accountability, school cultures are changing significantly with expectations of personal recognition, satisfaction and professional growth more than ever before likely to depend on the quality of teachers' experience within small task groups and the degree of 'empowerment' and 'ownership' provided by their colleagues at intermediate and senior management levels in schools.

Recent trends in leader–follower relationships

Handy's assertion (1993) that 'leadership has a dated air about it. It smacks of trench warfare and imperial administration . . . raises spectres of elites and privileged classes' reflects many enduring assumptions about the concept of leading others. Although outmoded in the realities of daily experience, there is still a sense in which traditional views of leadership suggest intellectual superiority, wisdom and greater freedom to use executive power than others possess.

However, more recent research suggests that these traditional views of leadership are in serious need of revision. For example, recent research by Kelley (1992) indicates that as a wide generalization even outstanding leaders contribute no more than about 20 per cent to the success of most organizations, with at least 80 per cent being provided by other members. Kelley and others assert that changing requirements for organizational success involve, *inter alia*, rejection of the myth of the 'great person', a demand for personal autonomy, more loosely structured work organization and practice through specialization, complexity and greater variety among individuals. Together with a reduction in numerical size of the workforce, all these trends increase expectations for independence, ownership of work processes and perceptions of self-worth among employees.

These developments have placed a premium on recent interpretations and styles of leadership. *Managing* and *leading* are *not* interchangeable terms. The status, power and authority involved in managing or leading processes are derived from different sources. In a managing activity, status, power and authority are derived essentially from the designated organizational position of the holder of an appointment. These are commonly seen in the relative hierarchical positions held, the degree of control over others and line-accountability defined in the job description and delineated through organizational rules and procedures. Frequently, and especially in education, they are also linked with stable, tenured positions. However, in the activity of leading, there is no requirement for direct links with formal status, designated appointment or the authority of 'office'. Thus, leadership rests on 'the power to influence the thinking and behaviour of others to achieve *mutually* desired objectives' (Williams, 1989, p. 24).

Both managing and leading are essentially processes that depend on different perceptions of relationships with others. Managing or leading comprise distinctively different behaviours which are reflected in the perceptions of people who experience them. In managing, there is a designated positional relationship dependent on relative formal status. The relationship is amenable to impersonal, prescriptive and task achievement requirements, with conformity focused on rewards for compliance and sanctions available for uncooperative behaviour. It is a controlling relationship resting on the realities of degrees of power and authority vested in differences in designated status positions between managers and subordinates.

Contrastingly, the relationship between leaders and followers is an umbilical one: 'the essential understanding ... is a simple one, but often overlooked or ignored: that leaders cannot exist without followers' (Williams, 1989, p. 24). Without the power or authority of formal, positional status, the relationship is always dependent on the willing acquiescence of the followers arising from a continuous and voluntary two-way interactive process – in itself suggestive of the possibility of impermanence. Leading is an accorded status not an appointed one. Leadership power and authority have to be *earned* from followers – sometimes through the 'vision' offered by the leader but more prosaically in organizations through patient negotiation involving the perceived needs of followers for recognition of their value, contribution or commitment to the enterprise: to derive personal job satisfaction and achieve personal status through undertaking tasks with the leader's support or approval. Thus, leadership is not simply a matter of one-way personal intuitive skills but requires conscious behaviour to secure the support of potential, or renew the support of existing, followers arising from a recognition that little can be achieved without attracting and sustaining the energies, commitment and enthusiasm of followers.

Of course, managers and leaders in all organizations including schools use both positional and earned authority in their activities on a daily basis. Some are intuitively successful but others use only positional authority in ways that are inappropriate in schools as professionally staffed organizations – often because they lack a clear perception of the fundamental differences between managing and leading colleagues. Accordingly, they lack the attitudinal stance and misjudge the quality of relationships required for effectiveness as leaders. Support is needed not only for enhancing personal leadership status but also, more importantly, to secure co-operative and positive contributions from followers in undertaking tasks required to achieve school objectives. For Covey (1989) and others such as Bennis and Nanus (1985), leadership is the primary personal priority: to decide *mutually* on what needs to be accomplished. Management is a second-order priority: how best to accomplish it. Sergiovanni (1992) believes 'we can do much to advance leadership by moving moral authority – the authority of felt obligations and duties derived from widely shared professional and community values, ideas and ideals – to center stage. To accomplish this goal, we must direct our efforts to create learning communities in each school. . . .'

Arguably, as teachers in schools are presumed to have largely homogeneous backgrounds through academic achievement, shared educational values and professional commitment in the progressive development of pupils, the more appropriate attitude is the leadership one. For example, those who hold management positions in schools may occupy more senior designated appointments but few, it is hoped, would lay claim to possessing superior values, intelligence, wisdom, experience or qualifications than those of their colleagues. Even fewer would be able to demonstrate these traditionally 'superior' virtues. The distinctive homogeneity of teachers as an occupational group and the emphasis on educational processes rather than 'products' of schooling suggest that the application of leadership principles rather than those of conventional institutional management is more appropriate for schools. Recent developments in theory and practice of leadership in schools point increasingly towards a development of a culture for collective educational purpose rather than earlier attitudes supporting the legitimacy of mere positional power (Torrington and Weightman, 1990; Sergiovanni, 1990).

Leaders and followers: the reciprocal relationship

A well-developed sense of collective purpose has been a distinctive feature of some schools for many years. Recent studies and research into that practice have illuminated ways in which it might be taken beyond intuitive and random existence (Caldwell and Spinks, 1988). The quotation from Drucker at the beginning of this chapter refers to the 'performance of people'. However, until relatively recently, the emphasis in management literature for school and in business applications has focused primarily on the performance of one person – the institutional 'leader'. Many widely read authors concentrate on the leader's role as visionary, innovator, strategist and people-centred. Others have emphasized the functions of chief executive roles in ways that suggest paranormal expectations of institutional leaders. Similarly, many management courses emphasize the development of institutional leaders and provide idealized models for students to adopt.

Somewhat fewer texts or management courses pay much attention to the majority of members in organizations and the significance of potential or existing followers or to their relationships with managers or leaders. Although misplaced, the reasons for not doing so are conventionally persuasive: the élitist tradition of the 'great leader' endures – much of it dependent on patriotic interpretations of 'heroes' in political and military history, classical mythology and 'epics' from Hollywood. Also stemming from this tradition is that 'followership' is perceived essentially as a submissive unthinking activity of powerless people – the 'sheep'. However, during the past few decades biographies of 'great leaders' have revealed major flaws in notions of superhuman powers possessed by leaders together with instances of subsequent disastrous effects arising from the behaviour of those who came to believe they were beyond human frailty.

In recent years, authors such as Burns (1978), Bennis (1987), Covey (1989), Kelley (1992) and Sergiovanni (1992) have indicated the importance of the contribution and influence of followers in the achievement of organizational objectives – and the importance of their 'empowerment' to successful enterprises. In many schools, teachers who respect and admire their headteachers would find it difficult to recognize in them many of the characteristics associated with leadership commonly listed in some management texts. They are more likely to be at ease with the Peters and Waterman's (1982) view of leadership:

> It is patient, usually boring coalition building. . . . It is altering agendas so that new priorities get enough attention. It is being visible when things awry and invisible when they are working well. It's building a loyal team at the top that speaks with more or less with one voice. It's listening carefully much of the time, frequently speaking with encouragement, and reinforcing words with believable action. It's being tough when necessary and it's the occasional use of naked power – or the 'subtle accumulation of nuances, a hundred things done a little better', as Henry Kissinger once put it. . . .

(p. 82)

Studies by Burns and others stress that leaders and followers must combine in the shaping of collective purpose. For example, the dilemma for Barber (1975) is that, on many occasions, when the combination is absent it is not so much a failure of leadership but rather the paucity or absence of shared values. An initial failure of leaders and followers to combine in the shaping of, and commitment to, mutually agreed values leads in turn to a consequential failure of popular will amongst followers on which leaders might draw for confident, secure knowledge of agreed collective purpose. However, positive interaction between leaders and followers leads to a clearer sense of mutual objectives, needs and motives than if they act separately. Thus, objectives emerge within a shared value system to which there is a mutual commitment and which, in turn, develops social relations through active participation within organizational structures designed to achieve them.

Followers as 'collaborative colleagues'

Recent concepts of role have clarified that becoming a leader is not simply a property to be acquired or an activity to be practised but is a values attitude through which a complex set of *relationships* with followers is developed leading to a merging of mutual purpose, needs, motives and activities. Linked with that attitude is a further realization that followers are not necessarily 'sheep' or 'apprentice leaders'. For most teachers, the daily reality in schools is that although explicit recognition of them as 'leaders' might be formally absent, they show initiative, make intelligent decisions, use value judgements, and are self-motivated for the benefit of pupils, their colleagues and the school community – almost invariably without having to refer to manuals on skills or technical rules of procedure. In doing so, they are undertaking the essential tasks of followers interpreted as *collaborative colleagues* in the completion of organizational work. This interpretation of the term 'follower' has contributed to a useful understanding of dynamic relationships with leaders. It provides a sense of collegial partnership in working together through value systems in cultures of mutually agreed collective purpose. Thus, leading and following are interdependent and essentially complementary. They are neither competitive nor submissive roles and are interchangeable according to situational requirements – typically found in work groups or task teams.

Research studies into the functioning of successful groups undertaken by Cartwright and Zander (1968), Belbin (1981) and Kelley (1992) have shown ways in which complementary and interchangeable roles in leading and following are adopted to achieve completion of tasks. For example, the functional team roles identified by Belbin clearly illustrate the ways in which followers become empowered to assume earned leadership roles in undertaking specific tasks within successful working groups. Similarly, from the perspective of followership, Kelley's work develops ideas about ways in which people choose to contribute to organizational achievement and success through clear understanding of various elective followership roles.

For both leaders and followers a key issue here is the need to understand the reasons why individuals choose to follow others. As yet the process is imperfectly understood but Kelley's recent work is useful in that it postulates several categories of followership, all shaped by personal considerations, preferences, existing relationships and previous experience. For Kelley, too many organizational leaders believe that charisma or vision is required from them to attract followers. In his view this is a simplistic and erroneous perception. In reality, many potential followers distrust charismatic leaders and visionaries. Some followers are motivated essentially through a personal desire of what it is they wish to achieve in their own lives and thus prefer leaders who function as facilitators in the achievement of objectives that enable followers to attain personal goals within organizational environments. Thus, Kelley's categories of followers include those influenced mainly by inter-personal relationships such as loyalty and camaraderie; those for whom career goals are important, e.g. apprentice leaders; others who seek self-meaning with an emphasis on vision or cause; and some who seek personal growth through discipleship and maturation. All represent deliberate choices not simply about careers or positional status but through making personal decisions about the quality and rewards of living a life compatible with personality and being at ease with oneself.

The value of research undertaken by Belbin, Kelley and others is that under varying circumstances many people *choose* to be followers; not because of perceived inadequacies, but from considerations arising from deliberate, considered and rational choices based on individual preferences and in recognition of the value of personal contribution. Organizational leaders who recognize, respect and value conscious choices made by potential followers learn to engage the talents, skills and experience of these 'elective followers' over a wide range of activities in contributing towards collective organizational effort and for mutual recognition of the *significance of that contribution to the follower* as well as to the work of the organization.

However, and unlike much of the published emphasis on leadership types and styles, the concept of the importance of 'elective followership' raises problems over recognition of the existence and motivation of those who are not traditional stereotypes – sheep, sycophants or acolytes. Mintzberg's belief (1973) that the effectiveness of a manager is dependent on the degree of personal insight into the requirements of role is equally applicable to an understanding of concepts of followership. For headteachers it calls for the reinforcement of established attitudes as professional leaders within complex relationships, rather than those engendered by manager–subordinate relationships.

Headteachers as professional leaders

In attempting to anticipate ways in which self-managing schools might more fully employ the individual and collective expertise, skills and experience of their professional staff – the most valuable, and expensive, resource available – it appears self-evident that headteachers should seek to develop their roles not as managers or chief executives of corporate activities but rather as professional leaders of talented and valued colleagues. Essentially, the leadership role of headteachers is to promote organizational change that seeks to build confidence and empower others through facilitating developments leading to more effectively fulfilling schools – for both pupils and their professional colleagues. In 1985, Bennis and Nanus' view of future effective leadership was that it would become more visible in organizations 'able to respond to spastic and turbulent conditions' (p. 18).

All schools in this country are working under conditions of discontinuous change. Traditional bureaucratic and hierarchical models of schools based on positional power are gradually being replaced by developing concepts about leadership which are concerned with collective purpose and earned authority. As in many other organizations there is little hard research evidence to indicate that a positive correlation between designated status and competence exists in education. Further, amongst teachers and others there is an enduring sense that schools are over-managed and under-led. Following the introduction of the National Curriculum, its assessment prescriptions and local management responsibilities, some schools have become preoccupied with administrative considerations and all these changes have served to reinforce impressions of developing managerial rather than educational school cultures.

Further, society is experiencing rapid change and, unsurprisingly, teachers reflect many of those changes. Just as society has become less tractable and accepting of designated positional power, teachers' attitudes have moved in similar directions. New perceptions and expectations of the legitimacy of independent thought, challenges of positional power and authority and developed self-esteem as active contributors in policy formulation and decision-making have replaced former perceptions of teachers as conformist, uncom-plainingly diligent, respectful of authority and offering unquestioning loyalty. A major task of headship during the next few years will be to recognize and accept the realities of societal change, and to capitalize on these developments as positive opportunities to create school cultures that will release the energies and talents of elective followers. The key relationships secured through leader-follower school cultures offer ways of achieving developments that lie beyond a manager–subordinate tradition.

The understanding of the need for new relationships implied in the leader–follower equation is not, in itself, a difficult concept to grasp. However, achiev-ing the reality of creating these relationships will be less easy to accomplish. The essential requirement here is for preparation and training – unlikely to succeed merely via formal, theoretical courses and conferences but more realistically through working daily along pathways towards new relationships in organizational behaviour. It is relatively easy to devise modified formal structures but considerably more difficult to develop new attitudes necessary for their effective working.

A further glimpse of the importance of perceiving leading and following as a centrally important relationships process is revealed in a variety of studies on headteachers and their roles undertaken during the past decade of mandated change. For example, the findings of Everard (1986), Hall *et al.* (1986), Weindling and Earley (1987), Jones (1988) and Sayer and Williams (1989) all indicate headteacher preoccuptions with 'people'. In these studies, the enduring emphasis is on matters concerned with ways in which headteachers might be assisted in sharing the institutional leader role with their colleagues in schools. Recurrent themes are: the management of delegation, motivation, innovation, empowerment, external relations and a variety of 'technical' matters such as strategic planning, curriculum analysis and resource management.

Earlier studies during the past twenty years or so have attempted to encapsulate the role of the headteacher through broadly seeking to categorize it variously as 'leading professional', 'chief executive' or 'senior teacher'. Following the recent unprecedented changes and the unavoidable requirement substantially to re-focus on the complexities of new responsibilities in even more demanding expectations of headteachers, it is hoped that during the next few years further developments in perceptions of the role will lead to a characterization of the headteacher as that of *professional leader*. The term attempts to convey a sense of unity of purpose through an emergent leader–follower dimension, and to reflect future demands from communities for 'educational leadership', especially following the decline of the LEA and the lacuna invariably found in politically motivated national policy utterances. It also suggests an understanding of new ways of collective working in that leaders cannot exist without followers; that it is a shared enterprise in an educational commitment for the benefit of all the members of communities served by schools.

Above all, 'professional leaders' seek to demonstrate the nature of the relationships involved – that leaders are in an indissoluble partnership with followers who elect to undertake, or accept, various roles in contributing to the life and work of schools. These roles are necessarily varied, not merely on the basis of differentiated positional status but also because of an understanding of when to offer leadership for the holistic achievement of school objectives and its integrated organizational development and when to follow others: for example, to follow on those occasions when the lead required is related to technical or other specialisms, teaching expertise and experience amongst colleagues or, and as importantly, through the exercise of personal choice.

Categories of followers: a tentative typology

The writer's own current preliminary study on identifying characteristics of 'followership' among experienced teachers in schools reflects similarities with those reported by Kelley (1992) in his research with employees in business organizations. For example, when asked about their individual contribution to both curriculum management and pupil progress in schools, several teachers clearly perceived personal roles as 'taking a lead' and although satisfied with their effort and success in those roles, resented being regarded as merely 'good teachers of their subjects'. In some instances, there appeared to be little explicit recognition of the high quality of their work, and virtually no praise for demonstrable achievement unless directly linked with public examination success of pupils. Respondents claimed that praise was offered sparingly – with success being attributed to abilities of pupils rather than to teaching effort and skill. Virtually no one reported examples of praise being given for the organization or management of curricular or pastoral activities at classroom or tutor-group levels.

Although taken from entirely different organizational and cultural environments, both studies show interesting similarities. The following section summarizes similarities and overlapping perceptions in categories of followers. As the writer's research is exclusively within the context of organizational change in self-managing schools, the following subheadings are those adopted by him in the continuing study. Because of some initial perceptual difficulties found in using the term 'follower' with respondents, the writer avoided direct use of the term in seeking to examine the nature and understanding of leader–follower relationships.

'Positive contributors'

This small group of respondents identified by the writer as 'positive contributors' are categorized as 'exemplary followers' by Kelley. In the writer's preliminary study, some respondents from schools indicated that independent thought and constructive criticism of proposed curricular or pastoral arrangements were welcomed by headteachers and senior colleagues. Their involvement as positive contributors to policies for school improvement, the sense of participating in collective planning and development, recognition of expertise and judgement and ownership of at least part of the process was both rewarding and personally developmental. However, a few others reported that independence in 'thinking otherwise' and suggestions for improvement tended to be regarded as unhelpful, obstructive and, on occasions, as deviant behaviour by more senior colleagues. Nevertheless, respondents in this sub-group were determined to continue to offer contributions because of personal confidence over their roles and commitment in taking initiatives to help the school to achieve its objectives. Importantly, they also recognized that patience was required if they were to succeed in being recognized as having a genuine contribution to make and not simply representing an interest-group or faction within the school. For them, the purpose of their involvement in collective effort was more important than personal frustration.

In Kelley's study, 'exemplary followers' are described as innovators, initiators, active participants and self-starters who assume ownership of both ideas and related activities. It appears that their leaders actively seek to harness and engage the talents and ideas of exemplary followers to achieve mutually agreed objectives. Exemplary followers are committed to the success of the organization, seek to complement the skills of the leader and willingly undertake some of the leader's tasks. Similarly, and as mentioned above, the value of some 'positive contributors' to schools was recognized by their colleagues, notably headteachers. Identified positive contributors justified confidence in them through transference of authority in discharging increasingly complex roles in self-managing schools. Recent examples of positive contributors in schools were evident in the delegation of financial control to departmental decision-making as budgetary cost-centres and through extending responsibilities for external relations to teachers other than the headteacher. In these ways, positive contributors clearly showed a sense of ownership of their tasks which, in turn, stimulated further commitment, initiative, experience and the acquisition of new skills closely matched to objectives and those activities required to achieve them. The quality of decisions made by respondents who subsequently implemented them, the sharpened sense of interdependence through working collaboratively and a willing acceptance of the realities of the effort required and personal accountability led to value-added outcomes.

Both studies revealed that where negative perceptions existed over the role of positive contributors (in the Williams study, found mainly at intermediate management levels in schools), some exemplary followers became alienated. Interestingly, Kelley's categories include 'the alienated follower' which he typifies as being perceived by other individuals as 'hostile', 'adversarial', 'cynical' but perceived by themselves as undervalued.

'Adversarial contributors'

This category provided the initial stimulus for the writer's preliminary study on LMS. As a result of several years' experience in the development of, and responsibilities for, schools it was clear that many initiatives in curriculum innovation in primary schools and organizational change in secondary schools were hindered or prevented through obstructive efforts by unco-operative teachers at all levels in schools. Even when fairly obvious failures by individuals to understand, accept and adopt appropriate strategies involved in the theory and practice of innovation were acknowledged and apparently overcome, residual problems remained in that some teachers continued to resist proposals for change. Part of the problem appeared to lie in the importance of understanding previously negative experiences of resistant teachers through their perceptions of self-worth and unsatisfactory relationships with colleagues – usually of senior positional status. The work of Gross *et al.* (1972) and Ball and Goodson (1985) on teachers' 'life histories' offered further possibilities for understanding individual resistance to change. Through a development of these perspectives, the writer identified the category of 'adversarial contributors'. Preliminary research amongst teachers suggests many similarities with Kelley's category of 'alienated follower'.

It is important to note that the category of adversarial contributors includes able teachers who for a variety of personal reasons had adopted antipathetic attitudes towards the ways in which schools were managed. Lacking confidence in the competence of senior colleagues, respondents were somewhat critical of efforts made by them and attempted to modify policies for change requiring their active participation but which had been unilaterally determined by 'senior management'. The reasons for disaffection were often complex but mainly involved perceptions of sustained personal and professional discourtesies. For example, those possessing relevant experience felt ignored by senior colleagues, appropriate existing skills were neglected, dishonest exploitation and manipulation by colleagues commonplace as were failures to create trusting relationships or honour promises. The withholding of essential information leading to an acute sense of disempowerment and being regarded as mere functionaries rather than intelligent valued colleagues in collective effort were also perceived as salient reasons for opposing policies and in shifts to adversarial contributions.

These negative perceptions in the writer's study are mirrored in the broader research undertaken by Kelley – hence his term 'alienated follower'. In addition, and common to both studies, most individuals who fell into this category could recall being 'positive contributors', but through various negative experiences – mostly over extended periods rather than single instances – had become either adversarial or withdrawn. Unsurprisingly, some teachers in the writer's survey were able to pinpoint particular schools and persons as being directly responsible for attitudinal change. Others attributed similar disappointments to the fact that, following success in one school, they had apparently failed to continue to enjoy similar achievements on moving to appointments in other schools. Invariably, these disappointments were attributed to serial professional and personal discourtesies at the hands of colleagues. Respondents' reactions to unhappy and unsuccessful experiences reflected bewilderment, sadness, frustration and anger that their energies had become geared to self-protective stratagems rather than to positive, satisfyingly contributive attitudes towards earlier commitment to school, pupils and career development.

'Compliant contributors'

Most organizations which are predominantly bureaucratic and hierarchical provide many rewards for conformity. So do schools. In the writer's study, the majority of respondents perceived themselves as conformists in that their preoccupations with teaching and many other responsibilities for the development of young people were preferable to expenditure of energy and time in politicking or guerrilla skirmishes within schools – unless, of course, it was necessary to defend the integrity of their objectives and tasks. Thus, most regarded themselves as team players rather than soloists, sought to avoid disruptive antagonisms with colleagues and wished to be allowed to undertake work in untroubled ways. They tended to accept the status quo and received wisdom willingly. The stability of school structures provided them with personal anchorages of security. For these respondents, high degrees of trust over personal integrity, planned development and competent management undertaken by senior colleagues were enduring expectations. Few claimed to be independent or constructively critical thinkers beyond their own specified roles, rarely questioning holistic school issues or wishing to be involved in them. For these respondents, such considerations were beyond their responsibilities. Generally, they were aware of the requirements of their job specifications and conscientiously sought to fulfil school expectations in undertaking appropriate tasks. All schools have teachers who are compliant contributors who give their energies willingly in carrying out duties in quietly confident and highly competent ways.

Nevertheless, in schools experiencing conditions of discontinuous change, it is questionable if traditionally compliant attitudes are entirely acceptable. 'Compliants' usually support existing policies and practice at the expense of personally independent and constructively critical attitudes. In the writer's study on schools, some teachers asserted that compliance was fostered by 'management' colleagues. The adoption of a more interventionist role towards matters such as whole-school policies or attempting to modify school routines would be considered as unhelpful, challenging and beyond one's positional 'station'. Kelley has important reservations about his 'conformist followers' in that under conditions of organizational instability and change they add little value to organizations if there is no development in and exercise of their personal capacities for independent thought and evaluative contribution. During the next few years, established attitudes of teachers as compliant contributors will need to be replaced under demands for new ways of active collaborative through positive contribution for future developments in self-managing schools.

'Minimalist contributors'

This category represents the stereotypical group of 'sheepish' followers. These were respondents in the writer's study who, for various reasons, appeared to have little or no understanding of, or sensitivity towards, the dynamic of daily collegial relationships. They appeared totally uninterested in the possibilities of examining, exploring or developing relationships and showed total acceptance of, or clear preference for, inert, passive rule-following regimes in schools. In the writer's study, very few teachers fell into this category. This was both an anticipated and a pleasing finding as it underlined previous studies and experience of the importance of an understanding by teachers of the significance of personally *earned* status for effectiveness in schools. The relatively few teachers in this category showed only marginal involvement in the life and work of the school, had little interest in pupils and contributed nothing beyond their contractual requirements.

In defence of attitudes and behaviour, most claimed they simply mirrored ways in which they were, or had been, consistently treated by senior colleagues. They asserted that in their schools, 'cultures of passivity' existed, particularly at departmental or faculty level, through deliberate refusal of delegation, conscious exclusion from decison-making, the withholding of essential information, being subjected to 'on the hoof' crisis-management decisions and experiencing despair over management incompetence. All these experiences were perceived as significant contributory reasons for minimalist responses. Thus, beyond routine teaching activities, minimalist contributors suggested they were mere spectators of wider events and developments in schools. Further, respondents bridled at the writer's suggestion that this was a self-elective indolent role. They asserted that earlier attempts to become involved in and to contribute to wider interests in their schools had been rejected or ignored – particularly evident for teachers appointed to part-time teaching posts. Similarly, Kelley's broader organizational studies suggest that recognition had been withheld by leaders and managers who had a low expectation of involvement by those perceived as 'passive followers'.

'Self-serving contributors'

Although gratified with the minuscule incidence of minimalist contributors in the initial study, the writer was somewhat surprised to find a substantial number of self-serving contributors. Following completion of the present study, it is intended to explore this category in greater detail as it may reflect cultural shifts within specific school contexts in response to contemporary legislative reform and recent changes in managerial styles.

Self-serving contributors are essentially pragmatists – an organizational species identified by Kelley as 'pragmatist followers'. At the core of their value systems is followership to promote self-interest through playing political games, using adventitious short-term organizational expedients and manipulating colleagues to gain personal advantage. Their brows are never furrowed with concerns about holistic considerations or the organizational development of their schools. Altruism never stains their thinking and although membership of a team might be personally important, positive contribution to its success is never a commitment.

When it is to personal advantage, self-serving contributors are adept at blending many, if not all, follower characteristics. For example, they play games in supporting the leader with ambivalent mixtures of independent thinking and judicious conformity. In the writer's study, decisions made by senior colleagues were criticized by respondents but implemented when it was personally advantageous, not least in order to avoid confrontation with, or criticism from, others. If problems existed, or risk assessment was high, respondents appeared to show considerable skill in avoiding early involvement but were available to salvage matters, invariably when it was to personal advantage. It appeared that relationships cultivated by self-serving contributors were calculated and transactional and that schools existed as mechanisms for personal success. Although of ostensible support to some leaders, the conclusion reached was that self-serving contributors added little of genuine value to the life and work of their schools and in many ways undermined attempts to foster and sustain relationships involving mutual trust, collegiality and collaborative endeavour. Further, so much organizational time and energy were devoted to micro-political activity and manipulation of information, events and colleagues that it appeared doubtful if positive outcomes from self-serving contributors could be beyond the mediocre.

Much more serious are the negative effects such people may have on their colleagues. The debilitating effects arising from expenditure of time and energy by others in counteracting the influence of self-serving contributors through diversion of valuable resources is a severe but often overlooked application of the principle of opportunity-costs. Schools, as labour-intensive organizations have to absorb heavy, and largely invisible, costs in human resources when activities of self-serving contributors are significant and permeate the management of schools. The expenditure in staff time and effort in counteracting activities of self-serving teachers is unquestionably much greater than in overcoming difficulties arising from adversarial, compliant and minimalist contributors.

Leading and following in self-managing schools

The previous section presented a review of broad categories of followers identified within a preliminary study of leader–follower relationships. The majority of secondary schools experience complex webs of interpersonal relationships on a daily basis in coping with the realities of organizational behaviour. The purpose of this section is to suggest ways, rather than prescribe methods, in which different interpretations of concepts of 'followership' might be used to consider strategies to achieve enhanced collaborative, co-operative and positive relationships other than those traditionally used to 'control' and 'promote' the management of schools through conventionally hierarchical, designated status frameworks.

As professionally staffed organizations under increasingly complex operating conditions, self-managing schools will be required to develop more flexible levels of authority based on 'earned' leadership rather than through conventional positional status on which formal management of schools has been traditionally based. It is self-evident that the ways in which schools are governed and required to operate have already changed significantly since the legislation of 1988 and 1993. Therefore, the management of organizational structures and behaviour will inevitably change in response to new external and internal expectations.

In responding to the many new requirements it is essential to acknowledge and capitalize on a truism that perceptions of an ability to 'lead' are held by almost everyone. The degree to which such perceptions are valid can be measured only following practical experience. In self-managing schools it is *the* management task to provide opportunities for all teachers to contribute their experience, abilities and skills across the full range of activities including those hitherto regarded as domains of 'senior management', e.g. development planning, financial control and external relations. If leadership in schools is to become a generalized living reality and not merely the preserve of 'senior people', there will, of course, be a requirement for training in appropriate roles, skills and practical opportunities to gain experience for all teachers. An essential priority for self-managing schools is the development of an attitude towards leadership that it is an 'earned' role independent of formal status and accorded by followers: not secured through appointed or designated status. Where held, appointed status and earned status is a most powerful combination because of the many opportunities available to harness commitment to shared values, holistic objectives and the resources to achieve them. In effect, it provides both the authority to define collective ends and the authority to deploy individual and group follower commitment as the means to achieve the declared objectives. Thus, a crucially important matter for self-managing schools will be recognition that the real source of power in leader–follower relationships is held by the followers – whether they are teachers, parents or members of the community. In its various forms, followership arises naturally from a sense of shared purpose. It is sustained through intrinsic satisfactions such as achievement and in mutual recognition of the value of differentiated contributions made by individuals and groups to the success of collective effort.

Unequivocally, the literature of education management reveals there is much yet to be accomplished in the running of schools. Obviously, a school is more than a group of classrooms held together by a common heating system or a group of entrepreneurs (teachers) surrounded by parking space (Murphy in Reynolds and Cuttance, 1992). More importantly, it is also clear that some headteachers appear unable to win the confidence or trust of their colleagues. There are deputy headteachers who, as 'headteachers in waiting', assert that valuable learning in preparation for headship arises from serving with colleagues who provide negative role models. Many middle managers do not enjoy the trust or confidence of their peers, junior colleagues or headteachers. Teachers at all levels feel threatened by some exceptionally able colleagues and thus ignore or under-use valuable talents beneficial to the school and pupils.

All these, and other similar, organizational problems are well documented in the literature and commonly found in the folklore of schools. They underline the necessity to develop new attitudes in the management of effective self-managing schools. Murphy (1992) emphasizes the importance of resolving such problems: 'Perhaps the most important and enduring lesson from all the research on effective schools is that the better schools are more tightly linked – structurally, symbolically and culturally – than the less effective ones. They operate more as an organic whole and less as a loose collection of disparate sub-systems' (p. 168). Reynolds and Packer (1992) are more explicit: 'We have concentrated, to put it simply, upon the first dimension of schooling – the formal, reified, organizational structure – without looking in enough detail at the second – *cultural and informal* – *world of values, attitudes and perceptions, which together with the third dimension – the complicated web of personal relationships within schools* – will determine a school's effectiveness or ineffectiveness (*emphasis added*) (p. 178). The words emphasized in the quotation represent in the opinion of the writer the most pressing priority for self-managing schools during the next few years. It is not simply a question of choice among 'first dimension' priorities such as undertaking responsibilities for enhancing curriculum and assessment quality through astute resource-matching within severe personnel and budgetary constraints or the development of public relations in a 'market' climate. These are the requirements of successful management and are immediate concerns, but the 'immediate' should not be permitted to conceal the longer-term requirements of schools. The argument throughout this chapter is that attention is urgently required for the development of the second and third 'dimensions' of effective schools. It is these that will serve, underpin and enhance the quality of the first 'dimension' of conventional practice in schooling. And it is here that the Drucker assertion at the beginning of this chapter reflects the key concept for headteachers and their colleagues. Headteachers who will be considered as effective leaders of schools a decade from now are certain to perceive their roles very differently from those currently serving. They will be much more aware of the importance of human resource management than preoccupations with material and fiscal resource management of their predecessors a decade earlier – simply because the preparation, experience and 'models' for headship will have changed. Important elements providing a basis for that opinion lie in the work of many researchers such as Elliot *et al.* (1981), Belbin (1981), Goodlad (1984), Handy (1993), Reynolds (1985), Reynolds *et al.* (1987) and Fullan (1991).

Arising from small-scale longitudinal studies by the writer (Williams, 1979, 1981, 1985, 1989, 1992 and current), it is held that earlier notions about leaders and followers require considerable revision. Followers do not require patronizingly unilateral prescriptions about 'liberating', 'empowering', 'inspiring' or 'enlightening' provided by 'democratic' managers or leaders. Rather, what is now required is that managers and leaders dismantle traditional notions about positional 'authority', presumed 'wisdom' of status and the shrine of extensive 'experience'. These ideas, largely derived from bureaucratic organizational stereotypes, should be replaced by an evolving sense of the reality that followership is not a matter of automatic status associated with designated subordinate positions within a formal hierarchy. Unlike limited choices open to subordinates, followers voluntarily make considered decisions about their roles. Without making a conscious choice to follow, they are unlikely to provide whole-hearted effort and commitment in their work. From the writer's initial study, outline criteria emerged which suggest that respondents were encouraged to make voluntary choices over positive contributor roles in circumstances where personally rewarding conditions existed in their schools.

Of course, much more research and experience are required before clear criteria and working models will emerge but preliminary findings suggest the following are important in positive contributor–leader relationships:

- mutual credibility and secure confidence based on agreed values such as trust and integrity, honesty and commitment – all *earned* through existing and renewed competence;
- a sense of active and full partnership through clearly understood

and necessarily differentiated organizational roles and positional status;

- a sense of collective 'mission' or 'vision' that emerges through discussion and agreement within the partnership and becomes owned by everyone;
- clear, shared understanding of joint responsibility for both success and failure – viewed as collective learning processes;
- expectations of participation in, and accountability for, holistic objectives as well as for contributory specialist goals;
- a clear sense of *obligation* for – and commitment to – the sustained development of colleagues and pupils;
- involvement requiring everyone to be active contributors to improvement, and not simply as employees, through providing value-added increments towards school development.

For everyone involved in the life and work of self-managing schools the leader–follower relationship should become a reality embedded in their cultures. In such cultures the main objective should be to promote the development of everyone as *positive contributors* and to accept that on occasions obligations as elective followers may be more influential roles than 'leading' in the development of schools as communities of learners, followers and leaders. Because of the value systems existing in these cultures there should be no acceptance of, or agreement to, staff roles as spectators in self-managing schools in the future. All teachers should be encouraged to perceive themselves as positive contributors in leader–follower school cultures. That is the immediate core task of headteachers during the next few years and a crucial one in the preparation of headteachers responsible for significantly different forms of school organization during the next century when schools might not be held together by anything other than their value systems.

Conclusion

For headteachers as *professional leaders* of self-managing schools during the next few years and beyond, the real test of their leadership will not be the size of their following – many undesirable leaders can, and do, achieve impressive numerical support – but rather the test will lie in the quality of positive contributions made by followers to the development of more effective schools. These will be schools that are not merely efficient in business terms but effective in the ways in which all pupils are able, and are encouraged, to grow as autonomous individuals and who are supported by varied interests within communities served by their schools. To provide leadership worthy of high-quality followership involves careful consideration of the relationships through which it is offered together with a clear understanding of educational objectives and the ways in which they are to be achieved. Above all, earned leadership requires courage to sustain personal and collective integrity in a values system harnessed to educational purpose.

Current developments indicate that effective schools achieve their objectives through the co-ordinated efforts of individuals contributing to the exercise of collective leadership and followership. Effective schools will emerge only through sustained mutual endeavour, trust and confidence amongst leaders and followers. Thus, the central task for headteachers, as designated leaders of schools, is the active stewardship of a value system that continuously promotes and nurtures an *earned leadership* culture. Without the development of such attitudes and values in their daily experience, many teachers will not elect to follow and others might withdraw earlier support. It is also essential to acknowledge that it is followers who confer power upon leaders and, having done so, accept their responsibilities willingly and with commitment.

A significant yardstick for effective schools in future will be the degree to which they develop as communities of leaders for pupils, teachers and parents. To achieve this paramount objective, it will be necessary for headteachers and their colleagues to accept that *leading* and *following* are genuinely professional attitudes in collaborative interdependent endeavour and not simply a hastily bundled set of administrative or management skills. It is through the quality of the performance of many people within collective leader–follower relationships that success in schools will be achieved. This will emphatically *not* be achieved through organizational structures developed to control educational enterprise and professional initiatives through regulatory prescription designed to achieve organizational dependence under central government direction.

Bibliography

Alexander, K. and Williams, V. (1978) Judicial review of educational policy: the teachings of Tameside. *British Journal of Educational Studies* **26**(3).

Association of County Councils Audit Commission (1989) *Losing an Empire, Gaining a Role.* Occasional paper No. 10. December. London.

Association of County Councils Audit Commission (1993) *The Education Bill: Memorandum by the Local Authority Associations.* London.

Audit Commission (1992) *Getting in on the Act* (report of the Audit Commission/HMI). London: HMSO.

Ball, S. J. (1993) Education, Majorism and the curriculum of the dead. *Curriculum Studies* **7**(3).

Ball, S. J. and Goodson, I. F. (eds). (1985) *Teachers' Lives and Careers.* Lewes: Falmer Press.

Barber, B. (1975) Command performance. *Harper's Magazine* (April). New York.

Bash, L. and Coulby, D. (1989) *The Education Reform Act.* London: Cassell.

Batho, G. (1989) *Political Issues in Education.* London: Cassell.

Belbin, R. M. (1981) *Management Teams.* Oxford: Butterworth-Heinemann.

Benn, C. and Simon, B. (1972) *Halfway There* (second edition). Harmondsworth: Penguin Books.

Bennis, W. (1987) *Why Leaders Can't Lead.* San Francisco: Jossey Bass.

Bennis, W. and Nanus, B. (1985) *Leaders.* New York: Harper & Row.

Black, P. J. (1993) Formative and summative assessment by teachers. *Studies in Science Education* **21**, 49–97.

Bolton, E. (1992) The quality of teaching. In *Education: Putting the Record Straight.* London: Network Education Press.

Bondi, L. (1991) Choice and diversity in school education: comparing developments in the United Kingdom and the USA. *Comparative Education* **27**(2).

Brighouse, T. (1986) *Education* **165.**

Burns, J. M. (1978) *Leadership.* New York: Harper & Row.

Caldwell, B. J. and Spinks, J. M. (1988) *The Self-Managing School.* Lewes: Falmer Press.

Cartwright, D. and Zander, A. (eds) (1968) *Group Dynamics Research and Theory.* New York: Harper & Row.

Chitty, C. and Simon, B. (eds) (1993) *Education Answers Back.* London: Lawrence & Wishart.

Chubb, J. E. and Moe, T. M. (1990) *Politics, Markets and America's Schools.* Washington, DC: Brookings Institution.

Chubb, J. E. and Moe, T. M. (1992) *A Lesson in School Reforms from Great Britain.* Washington, DC: Brookings Institution.

Coleman, M., Bush, T. and Glover, D. (1993) Researching autonomous schools: a survey of the first 100 GM schools. *Educational Research* **35**(2).

Cooper, B. and West-Burnham, J. (1988) Management issues in the introduction of an appraisal scheme. In Fidler, B. (ed.) *Staff Appraisal in Schools and Colleges*. Harlow: Longman.

Covey, S. R. (1989) *The Seven Habits of Highly Effective People*. New York: Simon & Schuster.

Cox, C. B. and Dyson, A. E. (eds) (1969) *Fight for Education* and *The Crisis in Education*. London: Critical Quarterly Review.

Cox, C. B. and Dyson, A. E. (eds) (1970) Goodbye Mr Short. *Critical Quarterly Review.*

Department of Education and Science (DES) (1965) Circular 10/65. *The Organization of Secondary Education*. London: HMSO.

Department of Education and Science (DES) (1972) *Education; A Framework for Expansion* (White Paper). London: HMSO.

Department of Education and Science (DES) (1977a) *Education in Schools: A Consultative Document* (Cmd. 6869). London: HMSO.

Department of Education and Science (DES) (1977b) *A New Partnership for Our Schools* (The Taylor Report). London: HMSO.

Department of Education and Science (DES) (1980a) *A Framework of the Curriculum*. London: HMSO.

Department of Education and Science (DES) (1980b) *A View of the Curriculum*. London: HMSO.

Department of Education and Science (DES) (1981) *The School Curriculum*. London: HMSO.

Department of Education and Science (DES) (1983) *Teaching Quality* (White Paper) (Cmd. 8836). London: HMSO.

Department of Education and Science (DES) (1984) *Slow Learners and Less Successful Pupils in Secondary Schools*. London: HMSO.

Department of Education and Science (DES) (1985a) *Better Schools* (White Paper). London: HMSO.

Department of Education and Science (DES) (1985b) *The Curriculum from 5 to 16*. London: HMSO.

Department of Education and Science (DES) (1985c) *Quality in Schools: Evaluation and Appraisal*. London: HMSO.

Department of Education and Science (DES) (1987a) *Financial Delegation to Schools: Consultation Paper*. London: HMSO.

Department of Education and Science (DES) (1987b) *Grant Maintained Schools: Consultation Paper*. London: HMSO.

Department of Education and Science (DES) (1988) *Local Management of Schools*. London: HMSO.

Department of Education and Science (DES) (1990a) *Burntwood School*. A report by HMI. 12–16 November. Reference 105/91/S2.

Department of Education and Science (DES) (1990b) *Aspects of Education in the USA: Teaching and Learning in New York City Schools: A paper by Her Majesty's Inspectorate*. London: HMSO.

Department of Education and Science (DES) (1991) Circular 12/91. *School Teacher Appraisal*. London: HMSO.

Department of Education and Science (DES) (1992) *School Governors: A Guide to the Law*. London: HMSO.

Department for Education (DFE) (1992) *Choice and Diversity. A New Framework for Schools*. London: HMSO.

Drucker, P. (1980) *Management*. London: Pan Books.

Elliott, J., Bridges, D., Ebbutt, D., Gibson, R. and Nias, J. (1981) *School Accountability.* London: Grant McIntyre.

Everard, K. B. (1986) *Developing Management in Schools.* Oxford: Blackwell.

Fullan, M. (1991) *The New Meaning of Educational Change.* London: Cassell.

(*The*) *Future of Education in Wandsworth. The Post American Study Tour Position.* (1990) A report to Wandsworth Education Committee, April.

Gardner, H. (1983) *Frames of Mind.* New York: Paladin Books.

Goodlad, J. I. (1984) *A Place Called School.* New York: McGraw-Hill.

Gretton, J. and Jackson, M. (1976) *William Tyndale: Collapse of a School – or a System?* London: George Allen & Unwin.

Gross, N., Giacquinta, J. B. and Bernstein, J. (1972) *Implementing Organizational Innovations.* London: Harper & Row.

Hall, V., Mackay, H., and Morgan, C. (1986) *Head Teachers at Work.* Milton Keynes: Open University Press.

Handscomb, G. (1991) LMS rhetoric reality. *Education,* 9 August.

Handy, C. (1993) *Understanding Organisations* (4th edition). Harmondsworth: Penguin Books.

Hansard, House of Commons, 20 November 1987

Hargreaves, D. H. (1982) *The Challenge for the Comprehensive School.* London: Routledge & Kegan Paul.

Hargreaves, D. H. and Hopkins, D. (1991) *The Empowered School.* London: Cassell.

Hargreaves, D. H. *et al.* (1992) *Development Planning: A Practical Guide.* London: DES.

Independent, The, Report on parents' surveys, 10 May 1993.

Jay, A. (1981) Foreword to Belbin, R. M., *Management Teams.* Oxford: Butterworth-Heinemann.

Jones, A. (1988) *Leadership for Tomorrow's Schools.* Oxford: Blackwell.

Kelley, R. E. (1992) *The Power of Followership.* New York: Doubleday.

Kogan, M. (1971) *The Politics of Education.* Harmondsworth: Penguin Books.

Lawrence, I. (1992) *Power and Politics at the Department of Education and Science.* London: Cassell.

Locke, M. (1974) *Power and Politics in the School System: A Guidebook.* London: Routledge & Kegan Paul.

Maclure, J.S. (1989) *Education Re-formed* (second edition). London: Hodder & Stoughton.

Mann, J. (1979) *Education.* London: Pitman.

Mintzberg, H. (1973) *The Nature of Managerial Work.* New York: Harper & Row.

Morgan, V., Dunn, S., Cairns, E. and Fraser, G. (1993) How do parents choose a school for their child? An example of the exercise of parental choice. *Educational Research* 35(2).

Morris, R. (ed.) (1990) *Central and Local Control of Education after the Education Reform Act, 1988.* London: Longman.

Murphy, J. (1992) Effective schools: legacy and future directions. In Reynolds, D. and Cuttance, P. (eds) (1992) *School Effectiveness.* London: Cassell.

Murray, M. (1992) The CBI view: putting individuals first. In *Education: Putting the Record Straight.* London: Network Education Press.

National Commission on Education (1993) *Learning to Succeed.* London: Heinemann.

National Co-ordinating Committee on Learning and Assessment (NCCLA) (1993a) *Purposes of Learning and Assessment.* Middleton Cheney: NCCLA.

National Co-ordinating Committee on Learning and Assessment (NCCLA) (1993b) *Educational Problems with Key Stage 3 Testing.* Middleton Cheney NCCLA.

National Co-ordinating Committee on Learning and Assessment (NCCLA) (1993c) *A Reconstructed National System, Partnerships for the 21st Century.* Middleton Cheney NCCLA.

National Curriculum Council (1993) *Teaching Science at Key Stage 3 and 4.* London: HMSO.

National Curriculum Council/Schools Examinations and Assessment Council (1993) *The National Curriculum and Its Assessment: An Interim Report.* London: HMSO.

Organization for Economic Co-operation and Development (OECD) (1975) *Review of National Policies for Education: Educational Development Strategy in England and Wales.* Paris: OECD.

Peters, T. J. and Waterman, R. H. (1982) *In Search of Excellence.* New York: Harper & Row.

Pile, Sir W. (1979) *The Department of Education and Science.* London: George Allen & Unwin.

Plaskow, M. (ed.) (1985) *Life & Death of the Schools Council.* Lewes: Falmer Press.

Ranson, S. and Thomas, H. (1989) Education reform: consumer democracy or social democracy? In Stewart, J. and Stoker, G. *The Future of Local Government.* London: Macmillan.

Reich, R. B. (1991) *The Work of Nations.* New York: Knopf.

Reynolds, D. (ed.) (1985) *Studying School Effectiveness.* Lewes: Falmer Press.

Reynolds, D. and Cuttance, P. (eds) (1992) *School Effectiveness.* London: Cassell.

Reynolds, D. and Packer, A. (1992) School effectiveness and school improvement in the 1990s. In Reynolds, D. and Cuttance, P. (eds) (1992) *School Effectiveness.* London: Cassell.

Reynolds, D., Sullivan, M. and Murgatroyd, S. (1987) *The Comprehensive Experiment.* Lewes: Falmer Press.

Richardson, R. (1988) *Re-organisation by Amalgamation.* London: Inner London Education Authority.

Sayer, J. and Williams, V. (eds) (1989) *Schools and External Relations: Managing the New Partnerships.* London: Cassell.

Scholey, F. T. (1990) Research paper for the University of Leicester and Northamptonshire County Council, p. 25.

Sergiovanni, T. J. (1990) *The Principalship.* Boston: Allyn and Bacon.

Sergiovanni, T. J. (1992) *Value-added Leadership.* New York: Harcourt Brace, Jovanovich.

Smith, P. B. and Peterson, M. F. (1988) *Leadership, Organisations and Culture.* London: Sage Publications.

Stevens, D. B. (ed.) (1991) *Under New Management.* Harlow: Longman.

Taylor, G. and Saunders, J. B. (1976) *The Law of Education.* London: Butterworths.

Times Educational Supplement, The (TES) (1976) Report, 22 October.

Times Educational Supplement, The (TES) (1992) Letters column, September–October.

Torrington, D. and Weightman J. (1990) *The Reality of School Management.* Oxford: Blackwell.

Wandsworth Education Committee (1992) *Diversity and Choice.* Wandsworth: Education Department.

Weindling, D. and Earley, P. (1987) *Secondary Headship: The First Years.* Windsor: NFER-Nelson.

West, A. (1992) Factors affecting choice of school for middle class parents. *Education Management and Administration* **20**(4).

Whitty, G., Edwards, T. and Gewirtz, S. (1993) *Specialisation and Choice in Urban Education: The City Technology Experiment.* London: Routledge.

Williams, V. (1976) Local education authorities and continuity of educational provision. *Trends in Education,* 1976, issue 1.

Williams, V. (1979) A framework for consideration. In Sayer, J. (ed.) *Staffing Our Secondary Schools.* London: Secondary Heads Association.

Williams, V. (1981) *Leadership – A Developing Perspective.* Oxford: OUDES occasional paper.

Williams, V. (1985) *Accountability in Education: Public Confidence and Professional Development?* Oxford: OUDES occasional paper.

Williams, V. (1989) Schools and their communities: issues in external relations. In Sayer, J.

and Williams, V. (eds) (1989) *Schools and External Relations: Managing the New Partnerships.* London: Cassell.

Williams, V. (1992) Foreword to Alexander, K. and Williams, V. (eds) *Reforming Education in a Changing World.* Blacksburg VA: JEF.

Name index

Subject index